MW00885672

The Easy

Crock Pot Cookbook

for Beginners

Improve Your Daily Meals with 2000+ Days of Simple, Blanced & Healthy Recipes | Incl. A No-Stress 30-Day Meal Plan

Ruth C. Jackson

All Rights Reserved.

The contents of this book may not be reproduced, copied or transmitted without the direct written permission of the author or publisher. Under no circumstances will the publisher or the author be held responsible or liable

for any damage, compensation or pecuniary loss arising directly or indirectly from the information contained in this book.

Legal notice.

This book is protected by copyright. It is intended for personal use only. You may not modify, distribute, sell, use, quote or paraphrase any part or content of this book without the consent of the author or publisher.

Notice Of Disclaimer.

Please note that the information in this document is intended for educational and entertainment purposes only. Every effort has been made to provide accurate, up-to-date, reliable and complete information. No warranty of any kind is declared or implied. The reader acknowledges that the author does not engage in the provision of legal, financial, medical or professional advice. The content in this book has been obtained from a variety of sources. Please consult a licensed professional before attempting any of the techniques described in this book.

By reading this document, the reader agrees that in no event shall the author be liable for any direct or indirect damages, including but not limited to errors, omissions or inaccuracies, resulting from the use of the information in this document.

CONTENTS

Appetizers Recipes

Lunch & Dinner Recipes

Poultry Recipes   32

Beef, Pork & Lamb Recipes   38

Fish & Seafood Recipes   44

Vegetable & Vegetarian Recipes   49

Side Dish Recipes 55

Soups & Stews Recipes 61

Snack Recipes 67

Dessert Recipes 73

APPENDIX A: Measurement Conversions   79

Appendix B : Recipes Index   81

Introduction

The Crock Pot, also known as a slow cooker, is a versatile kitchen appliance designed to make meal preparation simpler and more convenient. It works by cooking food at a low temperature over an extended period, allowing flavors to meld together and ingredients to become tender. The concept of slow cooking is rooted in traditional methods of preparing food over low heat for hours, but the Crock Pot brings this process into the modern age with user-friendly features and efficient design.

Benefits of Using a Crock Pot

Convenience: One of the most significant advantages of a Crock Pot is its convenience. You can prepare your ingredients, place them into the Crock Pot, set it, and let it cook while you go about your day. This "set it and forget it" approach is ideal for busy lifestyles, as you can return home to a hot, ready meal.

Time Efficiency: Although the Crock Pot cooks food slowly, it can save time in other ways. You can prepare meals in advance and let them cook while you work or handle other responsibilities. Additionally, slow cooking can be an efficient method for cooking tougher cuts of meat, which can become tender and flavorful with extended cooking times.

Enhanced Flavor: Slow cooking allows flavors to develop and meld over time, resulting in richer, more complex tastes. The low and slow heat breaks down ingredients and enhances their natural flavors, often making meals taste better than those cooked quickly.

Energy Efficiency: Crock Pots use less electricity than traditional ovens and stovetops. This can lead to lower energy bills and is an environmentally friendly option for cooking.

Healthier Meals: Slow cooking can help preserve nutrients in vegetables and other ingredients, leading to healthier meals. Moreover, the slow cooking process allows for the use of lean cuts of meat and less oil or fat, contributing to a healthier diet.

Versatility: Crock Pots are incredibly versatile and can be used to prepare a wide variety of dishes, including stews, soups, casseroles, roasts, and even desserts. Many recipes can be adapted for slow cooking, making it a valuable tool for any kitchen.

Using a Crock Pot: Tips and Tricks

Layer Ingredients Properly: To ensure even cooking, place dense, hard vegetables like potatoes and carrots at the bottom of the Crock Pot, as they take longer to cook. Place more delicate ingredients, such as fish or delicate vegetables, on top. This layering technique helps all ingredients cook evenly.

Avoid Overfilling: Fill the Crock Pot no more than two-thirds full. Overfilling can affect the cooking process and prevent food from cooking evenly. It can also cause spills and messes during cooking.

Use the Right Size: Choose a Crock Pot that matches the size of your meal. A larger Crock Pot can be beneficial for making large batches or meals for a family, while a smaller one is ideal for individuals or couples.

Don't Lift the Lid: Each time you lift the lid, heat and moisture escape, which can extend cooking times. Only lift the lid when necessary, such as when checking for doneness or adding ingredients.

Adjust Cooking Times: If you need to adjust the cooking time, you can switch between the high and low settings on the Crock Pot. Generally, cooking on the low setting for 8 hours is equivalent to cooking on the high setting for 4 hours. However, exact times may vary based on the recipe and ingredients.

Preheat the Crock Pot: For best results, preheat your Crock Pot for about 20 minutes before adding ingredients. This can help ensure a more consistent cooking temperature, especially if you're using the high setting.

Brown Meat First: While it's not always necessary, browning meat before adding it to the Crock Pot can enhance the flavor and texture of your dish. This step caramelizes the meat's surface, adding a deeper flavor to your meal.

Use Fresh Ingredients: For the best taste and texture, use fresh ingredients whenever possible. While frozen or canned ingredients can be convenient, fresh vegetables, herbs, and meats generally yield better results.

Cleaning and Maintenance of Your Crock Pot

Unplug and Cool: Before cleaning, always unplug the Crock Pot and allow it to cool completely. Cleaning it while still hot can be dangerous and may damage the appliance.

Remove Removable Parts: Most Crock Pots have a removable ceramic or metal insert. Remove this insert and wash it with warm, soapy water. This part is usually dishwasher safe, but always check the manufacturer's instructions to be sure.

Clean the Lid: The lid can usually be washed in the dishwasher or by hand with warm, soapy water. Make sure to thoroughly dry it before reattaching it to the Crock Pot.

Wipe the Base: The base of the Crock Pot, which contains the heating element, should not be submerged in water. Instead, wipe it down with a damp cloth. Avoid using abrasive cleaners or scrubbing pads that can damage the surface.

Remove Stubborn Stains: If you encounter stubborn stains or odors, try soaking the ceramic insert with a mixture of baking soda and water. For tougher stains, a paste made from baking soda and water can be applied directly to the stain. Let it sit for a while before scrubbing gently.

Store Properly: When storing your Crock Pot, ensure it is completely dry to prevent mold or mildew growth. Keep the appliance in a cool, dry place, and avoid stacking heavy items on top of it.

Check for Wear and Tear: Regularly inspect your Crock Pot for signs of wear or damage. Check the cord and plug for any fraying or other issues. If you notice any problems, it's best to discontinue use and seek repairs or replacement to ensure safety.

30 Day Meal Plan

DAY	BREAKFAST	LUNCH	DINNER
1	Greek Yogurt with Berries and Honey	Grilled Chicken Salad with Avocado	Jalapeno Chicken Wings 33
2	Oatmeal with Bananas and Almonds	Turkey and Hummus Wrap with Spinach	Fall Pork 39
3	Smoothie Bowl with Spinach, Pineapple, and Chia Seeds	Quinoa and Black Bean Salad	Chicken Stuffed With Beans 33
4	Scrambled Eggs with Spinach and Whole Grain Toast	Mediterranean Chickpea Salad	Oregano Pork Strips 39
5	Overnight Chia Pudding with Mango	Lentil Soup with a Side of Whole Wheat Bread	Green Chili Chicken 33
6	Whole Grain Pancakes with Fresh Berries	Avocado and Tuna Salad	Beef Sausages In Maple Syrup 39
7	Cottage Cheese with Pineapple and Walnuts	Chicken Caesar Salad	Harissa Chicken Breasts 34
8	Smoothie with Kale, Apple, and Protein Powder	Caprese Sandwich with Tomato, Basil, and Mozzarella	Saucy Beef Cheeks 40
9	Berry and Almond Butter Overnight Oats	Greek Salad with Feta and Olives	Chicken With Figs 34
10	Avocado Toast with a Poached Egg	Tomato Basil Soup with a Grilled Cheese Sandwich	Ginger And Rosemary Pork Ribs 39
11	Fruit Smoothie with Spinach and Greek Yogurt	Roasted Vegetable and Quinoa Bowl	Thyme Whole Chicken 34
12	Breakfast Burrito with Eggs, Beans, and Salsa	Turkey and Avocado Salad	Beef Heart Saute 40
13	Chia Seed Pudding with Berries	Spinach and Feta Stuffed Chicken Breast	Sweet Chicken Mash 36
14	Smoothie with Banana, Almond Milk, and Peanut Butter	Mediterranean Wrap with Hummus and Veggies	Chicken Wings And Mint Sauce 35
15	Greek Yogurt Parfait with Granola and Strawberries	Chicken and Avocado Wrap	Peppercorn Chicken Thighs 35

DAY	BREAKFAST	LUNCH	DINNER
16	Almond Flour Muffins with Blueberries	Black Bean and Corn Salad	Maple Ginger Chicken 35
17	Protein Pancakes with Maple Syrup	Quinoa Salad with Cucumber and Cherry Tomatoes	Easy Chicken Adobo 34
18	Smoothie Bowl with Mixed Berries and Nuts	Chicken and Vegetable Soup	Crockpot Cheeseburgers Casserole 40
19	Avocado and Tomato Breakfast Sandwich	Veggie and Hummus Wrap	Seasoned Poached Pork Belly 40
20	Oatmeal with Apple and Cinnamon	Greek Chicken Bowl with Feta and Olives	Barbacoa Beef 41
21	Smoothie with Berries and Spinach	Falafel Wrap with Tzatziki Sauce	Rosemary Pork 41
22	Yogurt with Granola and Honey	Lentil and Vegetable Stew	Lamb Shoulder With Artichokes 41
23	Chia Seed Pudding with Kiwi and Coconut	Grilled Vegetable Panini	Cheesy Pork Casserole 41
24	Egg White Omelette with Mushrooms and Spinach	Tuna Salad with Mixed Greens	Pork Sweet Potato Stew 42
25	Smoothie with Mango and Greek Yogurt	Chicken and Avocado Salad	Meatballs In Vodka Sauce 42
26	Overnight Oats with Peanut Butter and Banana	Vegetable Sushi Rolls	Seasoned Beef Stew 42
27	Cottage Cheese with Pineapple	Turkey and Vegetable Soup	Parmesan Rosemary Potato 43
28	Greek Yogurt with Fresh Fruit and Nuts	Quinoa and Chickpea Salad	Beef Roast With Cauliflower 43
29	Avocado Toast with Cherry Tomatoes	Mediterranean Chickpea Wrap	Thai Chicken 37
30	Smoothie with Spinach, Banana, and Almond Milk	Lentil Salad with Roasted Vegetables	Cola Marinated Chicken 37

Breakfast Recipes

Breakfast Recipes

Breakfast Butterscotch Pudding

Servings: 6
Cooking Time: 1 Hour And 40 Minutes

Ingredients:
- 4 ounces butter, melted
- 2 ounces brown sugar
- 7 ounces flour
- ¼ pint milk
- 1 teaspoon vanilla extract
- Zest of ½ lemon, grated
- 2 tablespoons maple syrup
- Cooking spray
- 1 egg

Directions:
1. In a bowl, mix butter with sugar, milk, vanilla, lemon zest, maple syrup and eggs and whisk well.
2. Add flour and whisk really well again.
3. Grease your Crock Pot with cooking spray, add pudding mix, spread, cover and cook on High for 1 hour and 30 minutes.
4. Divide between plates and serve for breakfast.

Nutrition Info:
- calories 271, fat 5, fiber 5, carbs 17, protein 4

Hot Eggs Mix

Servings: 2
Cooking Time: 2 Hours

Ingredients:
- Cooking spray
- 4 eggs, whisked
- ¼ cup sour cream
- A pinch of salt and black pepper
- ½ teaspoon chili powder
- ½ teaspoon hot paprika
- ½ red bell pepper, chopped
- ½ yellow onion, chopped
- 2 cherry tomatoes, cubed
- 1 tablespoon parsley, chopped

Directions:
1. In a bowl, mix the eggs with the cream, salt, pepper and the other ingredients except the cooking spray and whisk well.
2. Grease your Crock Pot with cooking spray, pour the eggs mix inside, spread, stir, put the lid on and cook on High for 2 hours.
3. Divide the mix between plates and serve.

Nutrition Info:
- calories 162, fat 5, fiber 7, carbs 15, protein 4

Chocolate Vanilla Toast

Servings: 4
Cooking Time: 4 Hrs

Ingredients:
- Cooking spray
- 1 loaf of bread, cubed
- ¾ cup brown sugar
- 3 eggs
- 1 and ½ cups of milk
- 1 tsp vanilla extract
- ¾ cup of chocolate chips
- 1 tsp cinnamon powder

Directions:
1. Cover the base of your Crock Pot with cooking spray.
2. Spread the bread pieces in the cooker.
3. Beat eggs with vanilla, milk, sugar, chocolate chips, and cinnamon in a bowl.
4. Pour this egg-chocolate mixture over the bread pieces.
5. Put the cooker's lid on and set the cooking time to 4 hours on Low settings.
6. Serve.

Nutrition Info:
- Per Serving: Calories 261, Total Fat 6g, Fiber 5g, Total Carbs 19g, Protein 6g

Potato Omelet

Servings:4
Cooking Time: 6 Hours

Ingredients:
- 1 cup potatoes, sliced
- 1 onion, sliced
- 6 eggs, beaten
- 2 tablespoons olive oil
- 1 teaspoon salt
- ½ teaspoon ground black pepper

Directions:
1. Mix potatoes with ground black pepper and salt.
2. Transfer them in the Crock Pot, add olive oil and cook on high for 30 minutes.
3. Then mix the potatoes and add onion and eggs.
4. Stir the mixture and cook the omelet on Low for 6 hours.

Nutrition Info:
- InfoPer Serving: 192 calories, 9.3g protein, 9.1g carbohydrates, 13.6g fat, 1.6g fiber, 246mg cholesterol, 677mg sodium, 285mg potassium

Broccoli Quiche

Servings:8
Cooking Time: 5 Hours

Ingredients:
- 2 tablespoons oatmeal
- 1 cup broccoli, chopped
- ½ cup fresh cilantro, chopped
- ¼ cup Mozzarella, shredded
- 1 teaspoon olive oil
- 8 eggs, beaten
- 1 teaspoon ground paprika

Directions:
1. Brush the Crock Pot bowl with olive oil.
2. In the mixing bowl mix oatmeal, eggs, and ground paprika.
3. Pour the mixture in the Crock Pot.
4. Add all remaining ingredients, gently stir the mixture.
5. Close the lid and cook the quiche for 5 hours on High.

Nutrition Info:
- InfoPer Serving: 80 calories, 6.3g protein, 2.2g carbohydrates, 5.3g fat, 0.6g fiber, 164mg cholesterol, 71mg sodium, 111mg potassium.

Buttery Oatmeal

Servings: 2
Cooking Time: 3 Hours

Ingredients:
- Cooking spray
- 2 cups coconut milk
- 1 cup old fashioned oats
- 1 pear, cubed
- 1 apple, cored and cubed
- 2 tablespoons butter, melted

Directions:
1. Grease your Crock Pot with the cooking spray, add the milk, oats and the other ingredients, toss, put the lid on and cook on High for 3 hours.
2. Divide the mix into bowls and serve for breakfast.

Nutrition Info:
- calories 1002, fat 74, fiber 18, carbs 93, protein 16.2

Potato Muffins

Servings:4
Cooking Time: 2 Hours

Ingredients:
- 4 teaspoons flax meal
- 1 bell pepper, diced
- 1 cup potato, cooked, mashed
- 2 eggs, beaten
- 1 teaspoon ground paprika
- 2 oz Mozzarella, shredded

Directions:
1. Mix flax meal with potato and eggs.
2. Then add ground paprika and bell pepper. Stir the mixture with the help of the spoon until homogenous.
3. After this, transfer the potato mixture in the muffin molds. Top the muffins with Mozzarella and transfer in the Crock Pot.
4. Close the lid and cook the muffins on High for 2 hours.

Nutrition Info:
- InfoPer Serving: 107 calories, 8g protein, 7.2g carbohydrates, 5.7g fat, 1.7g fiber, 89mg cholesterol, 118mg sodium, 196mg potassium

Creamy Strawberries Oatmeal

Servings: 8
Cooking Time: 8 Hours

Ingredients:
- 6 cups water
- 2 cups milk
- 2 cups steel cut oats
- 1 cup Greek yogurt
- 1 teaspoon cinnamon powder
- 2 cups strawberries, halved
- 1 teaspoon vanilla extract

Directions:
1. In your Crock Pot, mix water with milk, oats, yogurt, cinnamon, strawberries and vanilla, toss, cover and cook on Low for 8 hours.
2. Divide into bowls and serve for breakfast.

Nutrition Info:
- calories 200, fat 4, fiber 6, carbs 8, protein 4

Cheese Meat

Servings: 4
Cooking Time: 7 Hours

Ingredients:
- 10 oz ground beef
- 1 teaspoon minced garlic
- 1 cup Cheddar cheese, shredded
- ½ cup tomato juice
- 1 teaspoon chili powder
- 1 teaspoon olive oil

Directions:
1. Pour olive oil in the Crock Pot.
2. Add ground beef, minced garlic, tomato juice, and chili powder. Carefully mix the mixture.
3. Then top the meal with cheddar cheese and close the lid.
4. Cook the meal on low for 7 hours.
5. Carefully mix the meat before serving.

Nutrition Info:
- InfoPer Serving: 264 calories, 28.9g protein, 2.2g carbohydrates, 15.1g fat, 0.4g fiber, 93mg cholesterol, 311mg sodium, 398mg potassium

Cream Grits

Servings: 2
Cooking Time: 5 Hours

Ingredients:
- ½ cup grits
- ½ cup heavy cream
- 1 cup of water
- 1 tablespoon cream cheese

Directions:
1. Put grits, heavy cream, and water in the Crock Pot.
2. Cook the meal on LOW for 5 hours.
3. When the grits are cooked, add cream cheese and stir carefully.
4. Transfer the meal in the serving bowls.

Nutrition Info:
- InfoPer Serving: 151 calories, 1.6g protein, 6.9g carbohydrates, 13.2g fat, 1g fiber, 47mg cholesterol, 116mg sodium, 33mg potassium.

Chili Eggs Mix

Servings: 2
Cooking Time: 3 Hours

Ingredients:
- Cooking spray
- 3 spring onions, chopped
- 2 tablespoons sun dried tomatoes, chopped
- 1 ounce canned and roasted green chili pepper, chopped
- ½ teaspoon rosemary, dried
- Salt and black pepper to the taste
- 3 ounces cheddar cheese, shredded
- 4 eggs, whisked
- ¼ cup heavy cream
- 1 tablespoon chives, chopped

Directions:
1. Grease your Crock Pot with cooking spray and mix the eggs with the chili peppers and the other ingredients except the cheese.
2. Toss everything into the pot, sprinkle the cheese on top, put the lid on and cook on High for 3 hours.
3. Divide between plates and serve.

Nutrition Info:
- calories 224, fat 4, fiber 7, carbs 18, protein 11

Veggie Casserole

Servings: 8
Cooking Time: 4 Hours

Ingredients:
- 4 egg whites
- 8 eggs
- Salt and black pepper to the taste
- 2 teaspoons ground mustard
- ¾ cup milk
- 30 ounces hash browns
- 4 bacon strips, cooked and chopped
- 1 broccoli head, chopped
- 2 bell peppers, chopped
- Cooking spray
- 6 ounces cheddar cheese, shredded
- 1 small onion, chopped

Directions:
1. In a bowl, mix the egg white with eggs, salt, pepper, mustard and milk and whisk really well.
2. Grease your Crock Pot with the spray, add hash browns, broccoli, bell peppers and onion.
3. Pour eggs mix, sprinkle bacon and cheddar on top, cover and cook on Low for 4 hours.
4. Divide between plates and serve hot for breakfast.

Nutrition Info:
- calories 300, fat 4, fiber 8, carbs 18, protein 8

Bacon Potatoes

Servings:4
Cooking Time: 5 Hours

Ingredients:
- 4 russet potatoes
- 1 teaspoon dried thyme
- 4 teaspoons olive oil
- 4 bacon slices

Directions:
1. Cut the potatoes into halves and sprinkle with dried thyme and olive oil.
2. After this, cut every bacon slice into halves.
3. Put the potatoes in the Crock Pot bowl and top with bacon slices.
4. Close the lid and cook them for 5 hours on High.

Nutrition Info:
- InfoPer Serving: 290 calories, 10.6g protein, 33.9g carbohydrates, 12.8g fat, 5.2g fiber, 21mg cholesterol, 452mg sodium, 976mg potassium.

Quinoa Bars

Servings: 8
Cooking Time: 4 Hrs

Ingredients:
- 2 tbsp maple syrup
- 2 tbsp almond butter, melted
- Cooking spray
- ½ tsp cinnamon powder
- 1 cup almond milk
- 2 eggs
- ½ cup raisins
- 1/3 cup quinoa
- 1/3 cup almonds, toasted and chopped
- 1/3 cup dried apples, chopped
- 2 tbsp chia seeds

Directions:
1. Mix quinoa with almond butter, cinnamon, milk, maple syrup, eggs, apples, chia seeds, almonds, and raisins in a suitable bowl.
2. Coat the base of your Crock Pot with cooking spray and parchment paper.
3. Now evenly spread the quinoa-oats mixture over the parchment paper.
4. Put the cooker's lid on and set the cooking time to 4 hours on Low settings.
5. Slice and serve.

Nutrition Info:
- Per Serving: Calories 300, Total Fat 7g, Fiber 8g, Total Carbs 22g, Protein 5g

Orange Pudding

Servings:4
Cooking Time: 4 Hours

Ingredients:
- 1 cup carrot, grated
- 2 cups of milk
- 1 tablespoon cornstarch
- 1 teaspoon vanilla extract
- ½ teaspoon ground nutmeg

Directions:
1. Put the carrot in the Crock Pot.
2. Add milk, vanilla extract, and ground nutmeg.
3. Then add cornstarch and stir the ingredients until cornstarch is dissolved.
4. Cook the pudding on low for 4 hours.

Nutrition Info:
- InfoPer Serving: 84 calories, 4.3g protein, 10.8g carbohydrates, 2.6g fat, 0.8g fiber, 10mg cholesterol, 77mg sodium, 161mg potassium.

Morning Ham Muffins

Servings:4
Cooking Time: 2.5 Hours

Ingredients:
- 4 eggs, beaten
- 3 oz Mozzarella, shredded
- 3 oz ham, chopped
- 1 teaspoon olive oil
- 1 teaspoon dried parsley
- ½ teaspoon salt

Directions:
1. Mix eggs with dried parsley, salt, and ham.
2. Add mozzarella and stir the muffin mixture carefully.
3. Sprinkle the silicone muffin molds with olive oil.
4. After this, pour the egg and ham mixture in the muffin molds and transfer in the Crock Pot.
5. Cook the muffins on High for 2.5 hours.

Nutrition Info:
- InfoPer Serving: 168 calories, 15.1g protein, 1.9g carbohydrates, 11.1g fat, 0.3g fiber, 187mg cholesterol, 757mg sodium, 122mg potassium

Appetizers Recipes

Appetizers Recipes

Turkey Meatloaf

Servings: 8
Cooking Time: 6 1/4 Hours

Ingredients:
- 1 1/2 pounds ground turkey
- 1 carrot, grated
- 1 sweet potato, grated
- 1 egg
- 1/4 cup breadcrumbs
- 1/4 teaspoon chili powder
- Salt and pepper to taste
- 1 cup shredded mozzarella

Directions:
1. Mix all the ingredients in a bowl and season with salt and pepper as needed.
2. Give it a good mix then transfer the mixture in your Crock Pot.
3. Level the mixture well and cover with the pot's lid.
4. Cook on low settings for 6 hours.
5. Serve the meatloaf warm or chilled.

Stuffed Artichokes

Servings: 6
Cooking Time: 6 1/2 Hours

Ingredients:
- 6 fresh artichokes
- 6 anchovy fillets, chopped
- 4 garlic cloves, minced
- 2 tablespoons olive oil
- 1 cup breadcrumbs
- 1 tablespoon chopped parsley
- Salt and pepper to taste
- 1/4 cup white wine

Directions:
1. Cut the stem of each artichoke so that it sits flat on your chopping board then cut the top off and trim the outer leaves, cleaning the center as well.
2. In a bowl, mix the anchovy fillets, garlic, olive oil, breadcrumbs and parsley. Add salt and pepper to taste.
3. Top each artichoke with breadcrumb mixture and rub it well into the leaves.
4. Place the artichokes in your Crock Pot and pour in the white wine.
5. Cook on low settings for 6 hours.
6. Serve the artichokes warm or chilled.

Bacon Wrapped Chicken Livers

Servings: 6
Cooking Time: 3 1/2 Hours

Ingredients:
- 2 pounds chicken livers
- Bacon slices as needed

Directions:
1. Wrap each chicken liver in one slice of bacon and place all the livers in your crock pot.
2. Cook on high heat for 3 hours.
3. Serve warm or chilled.

Four Cheese Dip

Servings: 8
Cooking Time: 4 1/4 Hours

Ingredients:
- 1/2 pound fresh Italian sausages, skins removed
- 2 tablespoons olive oil
- 1 cup tomato sauce
- 1 cup cottage cheese
- 1 cup shredded mozzarella cheese
- 1/2 cup grated Parmesan cheese
- 1 cup grated Cheddar cheese
- 1/2 teaspoon dried thyme
- 1/2 teaspoon dried basil
- Salt and pepper to taste

Directions:
1. Heat the oil in a skillet and stir in the sausages. Cook for 5 minutes, stirring often then transfer the sausages in a Crock Pot.
2. Add the remaining ingredients and season with salt and pepper.
3. Cook on low settings for 4 hours.
4. The dip is best served warm.

Marinara Turkey Meatballs

Servings: 8
Cooking Time: 6 1/2 Hours

Ingredients:
- 2 pounds ground turkey
- 1 carrot, grated
- 1 potato, grated
- 1 shallot, chopped
- 1 tablespoon chopped parsley
- 1 tablespoon chopped cilantro
- 4 basil leaves, chopped
- 1/2 teaspoon dried mint
- 1 egg
- 1/4 cup breadcrumbs
- Salt and pepper to taste
- 2 cups marinara sauce

Directions:
1. Mix the turkey, carrot, potato, shallot, parsley, cilantro, basil, mint, egg and breadcrumbs in a bowl.
2. Add salt and pepper to taste and mix well.
3. Pour the marinara sauce in your Crock Pot then form meatballs and drop them in the sauce.
4. Cover the pot with its lid and cook on low settings for 6 hours.
5. Serve the meatballs warm or chilled.

Ranch Turkey Bites

Servings: 6
Cooking Time: 7 1/4 Hours

Ingredients:
- 2 pounds turkey breast, cubed
- 1 carrot, sliced
- 1/2 teaspoon garlic powder
- 1 tablespoon Ranch dressing seasoning
- 1 teaspoon hot sauce
- 1 cup tomato sauce
- Salt and pepper to taste

Directions:
1. Combine all the ingredients in a Crock Pot.
2. Mix well until the ingredients are well distributed and adjust the taste with salt and pepper.
3. Cover with a lid and cook on low settings for 7 hours.
4. Serve the turkey bites warm or chilled.

Marmalade Glazed Meatballs

Servings: 8
Cooking Time: 7 1/2 Hours

Ingredients:
- 2 pounds ground pork
- 1 shallot, chopped
- 4 garlic cloves, minced
- 1 carrot, grated
- 1 egg
- Salt and pepper to taste
- 1 cup orange marmalade
- 2 cups BBQ sauce
- 1 bay leaf
- 1 teaspoon Worcestershire sauce
- Salt and pepper to taste

Directions:
1. Mix the ground pork, shallot, garlic, carrot, egg, salt and pepper in a bowl.
2. Form small meatballs and place them on your working surface.
3. For the sauce, mix the orange marmalade, sauce, bay leaf, Worcestershire sauce, salt and pepper in your Crock Pot.
4. Place the meatballs in the sauce. Cover with its lid and cook on low settings for 7 hours.
5. Serve the meatballs warm.

Five-spiced Chicken Wings

Servings: 8
Cooking Time: 7 1/4 Hours

Ingredients:
- 1/2 cup plum sauce
- 1/2 cup BBQ sauce
- 2 tablespoons butter
- 1 tablespoon five-spice powder
- 1 teaspoon salt
- 1/2 teaspoon chili powder
- 4 pounds chicken wings

Directions:
1. Combine the plum sauce and BBQ sauce, as well as butter, five-spice, salt and chili powder in a crock pot.
2. Add the chicken wings and mix well until well coated.
3. Cover and cook on low settings fir 7 hours.
4. Serve warm or chilled.

Pimiento Cheese Dip

Servings: 8
Cooking Time: 2 1/4 Hours

Ingredients:
- 1/2 pound grated Cheddar
- 1/4 pound grated pepper Jack cheese
- 1/2 cup sour cream
- 1/2 cup green olives, sliced
- 2 tablespoons diced pimientos
- 1 teaspoon hot sauce
- 1/4 teaspoon garlic powder
- 1/4 teaspoon onion powder

Directions:
1. Combine all the ingredients in a Crock Pot.
2. Cover the pot with its lid and cook on high settings for 2 hours.
3. The dip is best served warm with vegetable sticks or bread sticks.

Molasses Lime Meatballs

Servings: 10
Cooking Time: 8 1/4 Hours

Ingredients:
- 3 pounds ground beef
- 2 garlic cloves, minced
- 1 shallot, chopped
- 1/2 cup oat flour
- 1/2 teaspoon cumin powder
- 1/2 teaspoon chili powder
- 1 egg
- Salt and pepper to taste
- 1/2 cup molasses
- 1/4 cup soy sauce
- 2 tablespoons lime juice
- 1/2 cup beef stock
- 1 tablespoon Worcestershire sauce

Directions:
1. Combine the molasses, soy sauce, lime juice, stock and Worcestershire sauce in your Crock Pot.
2. In a bowl, mix the ground beef, garlic, shallot, oat flour, cumin powder, chili powder, egg, salt and pepper and mix well.
3. Form small balls and place them in the sauce.
4. Cover the pot and cook on low settings for 8 hours.
5. Serve the meatballs warm or chilled.

Spicy Glazed Pecans

Servings: 10
Cooking Time: 3 1/4 Hours

Ingredients:
- 2 pounds pecans
- 1/2 cup butter, melted
- 1 teaspoon chili powder
- 1 teaspoon smoked paprika
- 1 teaspoon dried basil
- 1 teaspoon dried thyme
- 1/4 teaspoon cayenne pepper
- 1/2 teaspoon garlic powder
- 2 tablespoons honey

Directions:
1. Combine all the ingredients in your Crock Pot.
2. Mix well until all the ingredients are well distributed and the pecans are evenly glazed.
3. Cook on high settings for 3 hours.
4. Allow them to cool before serving.

Bourbon Glazed Sausages

Servings: 10
Cooking Time: 4 1/4 Hours

Ingredients:
- 3 pounds small sausage links
- 1/2 cup apricot preserves
- 1/4 cup maple syrup
- 2 tablespoons Bourbon

Directions:
1. Combine all the ingredients in your Crock Pot.
2. Cover with its lid and cook on low settings for 4 hours.
3. Serve the glazed sausages warm or chilled, preferably with cocktail sticks.

Rosemary Potatoes

Servings: 8
Cooking Time: 2 1/4 Hours

Ingredients:
- 4 pounds small new potatoes
- 1 rosemary sprig, chopped
- 1 shallot, sliced
- 2 garlic cloves, chopped
- 1 teaspoon smoked paprika
- 1 teaspoon salt

- 1/4 teaspoon ground black pepper
- 1/4 cup chicken stock

Directions:
1. Combine all the ingredients in your Crock Pot.
2. Cover with its lid and cook on high settings for 2 hours.
3. Serve the potatoes warm or chilled.

Three Cheese Artichoke Sauce

Servings: 16
Cooking Time: 4 1/4 Hours

Ingredients:
- 1 jar artichoke hearts, drained and chopped
- 1 shallot, chopped
- 2 cups shredded mozzarella
- 1 cup grated Parmesan
- 1 cup grated Swiss cheese
- 1/2 teaspoon dried thyme
- 1/4 teaspoon chili powder

Directions:
1. Combine all the ingredients in your Crock Pot.
2. Cover the pot with its lid and cook on low setting for 4 hours.
3. The sauce is great served warm with vegetable sticks or biscuits or even small pretzels.

Ham And Swiss Cheese Dip

Servings: 6
Cooking Time: 4 1/4 Hours

Ingredients:
- 1 pound ham, diced
- 1 cup cream cheese
- 1 can condensed cream of mushroom soup
- 1 can condensed onion soup
- 2 cups grated Swiss cheese
- 1/2 teaspoon chili powder

Directions:
1. Combine all the ingredients in a Crock Pot.
2. Cook on low settings for 4 hours.
3. Serve the dip preferably warm.

Beer Cheese Fondue

Servings: 8
Cooking Time: 2 1/4 Hours

Ingredients:
- 1 shallot, chopped
- 1 garlic clove, minced
- 1 cup grated Gruyere cheese
- 2 cups grated Cheddar
- 1 tablespoon cornstarch
- 1 teaspoon Dijon mustard
- 1/2 teaspoon cumin seeds
- 1 cup beer
- Salt and pepper to taste

Directions:
1. Combine the shallot, garlic, cheeses, cornstarch, mustard, cumin seeds and beer in your Crock Pot.
2. Add salt and pepper to taste and mix well.
3. Cover the pot with its lid and cook on high settings for 2 hours.
4. Serve the fondue warm.

Blue Cheese Chicken Wings

Servings: 8
Cooking Time: 7 1/4 Hours

Ingredients:
- 4 pounds chicken wings
- 1/2 cup buffalo sauce
- 1/2 cup spicy tomato sauce
- 1 tablespoon tomato paste
- 2 tablespoons apple cider vinegar
- 1 tablespoon Worcestershire sauce
- 1 cup sour cream
- 2 oz. blue cheese, crumbled
- 1 thyme sprig

Directions:
1. Combine the buffalo sauce, tomato sauce, vinegar, Worcestershire sauce, sour cream, blue cheese and thyme in a Crock Pot.
2. Add the chicken wings and toss them until evenly coated.
3. Cook on low settings for 7 hours.
4. Serve the chicken wings preferably warm.

Lunch & Dinner Recipes

Lunch & Dinner Recipes

Turnip And Beans Casserole

Servings:4
Cooking Time: 6 Hours

Ingredients:
- ½ cup turnip, chopped
- 1 teaspoon chili powder
- ¼ cup of coconut milk
- 1 teaspoon coconut oil
- ¼ cup potato, chopped 1 carrot, diced
- 1 cup red kidney beans, canned
- ½ cup Cheddar cheese, shredded

Directions:
1. Grease the Crock Pot bottom with coconut oil.
2. Then put the turnip and potato inside.
3. Sprinkle the vegetables with chili powder and coconut mil.
4. After this, top the with red kidney beans and Cheddar cheese.
5. Close the lid and cook the casserole on Low for 6 hours.

Nutrition Info:
- InfoPer Serving: 266 calories, 14.5g protein, 31.4g carbohydrates, 10g fat, 7.9g fiber, 15mg cholesterol, 113mg sodium, 742mg potassium.

Fennel Soup

Servings: 2
Cooking Time: 4 Hours

Ingredients:
- 2 fennel bulbs, sliced
- ½ cup tomatoes, crushed
- 1 red onion, sliced
- 1 leek, chopped
- 2 cups veggie stock
- ½ teaspoon cumin, ground
- 1 tablespoon dill, chopped
- ½ tablespoon olive oil
- Salt and black pepper to the taste

Directions:
1. In your Crock Pot, mix the fennel with the tomatoes, onion and the other ingredients, toss, put the lid on and cook on High for 4 hours.
2. Ladle into bowls and serve hot.

Nutrition Info:
- calories 132, fat 2, fiber 5, carbs 11, protein 3

Pinto Bean Sloppy Joes

Servings: 6
Cooking Time: 8 1/4 Hours

Ingredients:
- 2 tablespoons olive oil
- 2 carrots, sliced
- 1 shallot, chopped
- 4 garlic cloves, minced
- 1/2 teaspoon chili powder
- 1 cup dried pinto beans
- 2 red bell peppers, cored and diced
- 1 tablespoon balsamic vinegar
- 2 tablespoons tomato paste
- 1 cup diced tomatoes
- 2 cups water
- 1 small head green cabbage, shredded
- 1 cup frozen corn
- 1/2 teaspoon mustard seeds
- Salt and pepper to taste

Directions:
1. Heat the oil in a skillet and add the carrots, shallot and garlic and cook on low settings for 5 minutes.
2. Transfer in your crock pot and add the remaining ingredients.
3. Season with salt and pepper and cook on low settings for 8 hours.
4. Serve the dish warm or chilled.

Farro Pumpkin Stew

Servings: 6
Cooking Time: 6 1/4 Hours

Ingredients:
- 2 tablespoons butter
- 1 cup farro, rinsed
- 2 cups pumpkin cubes
- 1 shallot, chopped
- 1 garlic clove, minced
- 1/4 teaspoon cumin seeds
- 1/4 teaspoon fennel seeds
- 1/4 cup white wine
- 2 1/2 cups vegetable stock
- Salt and pepper to taste
- 1/2 cup grated Parmesan cheese

Directions:
1. Combine the butter, faro, pumpkin, shallot, garlic, cumin seeds, fennel seeds, wine and stock in your crock pot.
2. Add salt and pepper to taste and cook on low settings for 6 hours.
3. Serve the stew warm or chilled.

Lamb And Onion Stew

Servings: 2
Cooking Time: 8 Hours

Ingredients:
- 1 pound lamb meat, cubed
- 1 red onion, sliced
- 3 spring onions, sliced
- Salt and black pepper to the taste
- 1 tablespoon olive oil
- ½ teaspoon rosemary, dried
- ¼ teaspoon thyme, dried
- 1 cup water
- ½ cup baby carrots, peeled
- ½ cup tomato sauce
- 1 tablespoon cilantro, chopped

Directions:
1. In your Crock Pot, mix the lamb with the onion, spring onions and the other ingredients, toss, put the lid on and cook on Low for 8 hours.
2. Divide the stew between plates and serve hot.

Nutrition Info:
- calories 350, fat 8, fiber 3, carbs 14, protein 16

Apple Cherry Pork Chops

Servings: 6
Cooking Time: 3 1/4 Hours

Ingredients:
- 6 pork chops
- 4 red, tart apples, cored and sliced
- 1 cup frozen sour cherries
- 1/2 cup apple cider vinegar
- 1/2 cup tomato sauce
- 1 onion, chopped
- 1 garlic clove, minced
- 1 bay leaf
- Salt and pepper to taste

Directions:
1. Combine the pork chops, apples, sour cherries, tomato sauce, onion, garlic and bay leaf in your Crock Pot.
2. Add salt and pepper to taste and cook on high settings for 3 hours.
3. Serve the pork chops warm and fresh.

Indian Spiced Lentils

Servings: 6
Cooking Time: 6 1/4 Hours

Ingredients:
- 2 garlic cloves, chopped
- 1 sweet onion, chopped
- 2 tablespoons olive oil
- 1 cup red lentils, rinsed
- 1 sweet potato, peeled and cubed
- 1/2 teaspoon cumin powder
- 1/4 teaspoon chili powder
- 1/2 teaspoon turmeric powder
- 1/2 teaspoon garam masala
- 1 cup tomato sauce
- 2 cups vegetable stock
- 1/2 teaspoon grated ginger
- Salt and pepper to taste

Directions:
1. Combine the lentils and the remaining ingredients in your Crock Pot.
2. Add salt and pepper to taste and cook on low settings for 6 hours.
3. Serve the lentils warm.

3 Bean Chili

Servings: 6
Cooking Time: 8 Hours

Ingredients:
- 15 ounces canned kidney beans, drained
- 30 ounces canned chili beans in sauce
- 15 ounces canned black beans, drained
- 2 green bell peppers, chopped
- 30 ounces canned tomatoes, crushed
- 2 tablespoons chili powder
- 2 yellow onions, chopped
- 2 garlic cloves, minced
- 1 teaspoon oregano, dried
- 1 tablespoon cumin, ground
- Salt and black pepper to the taste

Directions:
1. In your Crock Pot, mix kidney beans with chili beans, black beans, bell peppers, tomatoes, chili powder, onion, garlic, oregano, cumin, salt and pepper, stir, cover and cook on Low for 8 hours.
2. Divide into bowls and serve for lunch.

Nutrition Info:
- calories 314, fat 6, fiber 5, carbs 14, protein 4

Cheddar Pork Casserole

Servings: 6
Cooking Time: 5 1/2 Hours

Ingredients:
- 2 tablespoons canola oil
- 2 large onions, sliced
- 1 1/2 pounds ground pork
- 1 carrot, grated
- 1 cup finely chopped mushrooms
- 1/2 cup hot ketchup
- Salt and pepper to taste
- 2 cups grated Cheddar

Directions:
1. Heat the canola oil in a frying pan and add the onions. Cook on low heat for 10 minutes until they begin to caramelize.
2. Transfer the onions in your Crock Pot. Add the pork, carrot, mushrooms and ketchup and mix well, adjusting the taste with salt and pepper.
3. Top with Cheddar cheese and cook on low settings for 5 hours.
4. Serve the casserole preferably warm.

Crock Pot Jambalaya

Servings: 8
Cooking Time: 6 1/2 Hours

Ingredients:
- 2 tablespoons olive oil
- 8 oz. firm tofu, cubed
- 1 large onion, chopped
- 2 red bell peppers, cored and diced
- 2 garlic cloves, chopped
- 1/2 teaspoon Cajun seasoning
- 2 ripe tomatoes, peeled and diced
- 1/2 head cauliflower, cut into florets
- 1 large sweet potato, peeled and cubed
- 1 tablespoon tomato paste
- 1 1/4 cups vegetable stock
- Salt and pepper to taste

Directions:
1. Heat the oil in a skillet and add the tofu. Cook on low settings for a few minutes until golden brown.
2. Transfer in your Crock Pot and add the rest of the ingredients, adjusting the taste with salt and pepper.
3. Cook on low settings for 6 hours.
4. Serve the jambalaya warm and fresh.

Cuban Flank Steaks

Servings: 6
Cooking Time: 8 1/4 Hours

Ingredients:
- 6 beef flank steaks
- 2 red onions, sliced
- 1 teaspoon cumin seeds
- 1 teaspoon chili powder
- 1 teaspoon dried oregano
- 1 cup beef stock
- 1 chipotle pepper, chopped
- 2 limes, juiced
- Salt and pepper to taste

Directions:
1. Combine the steaks in your Crock Pot and add salt and pepper.
2. Cover and cook for 8 hours on low settings.
3. Serve the steaks warm.

Greek Style Chicken Ragout

Servings: 8
Cooking Time: 8 1/4 Hours

Ingredients:
- 4 chicken breasts, halved
- 1 pound new potatoes, washed
- 1 pound baby carrots
- 1 zucchini, cubed
- 4 garlic cloves, chopped
- 1 sweet onion, sliced
- 4 artichoke hearts, chopped
- 1 lemon, juiced
- 1 teaspoon dried oregano
- Salt and pepper to taste
- 1 1/2 cups chicken stock

Directions:
1. Combine the chicken, potatoes, carrots, zucchini, garlic, onion, artichoke hearts, lemon juice, oregano and stock in your Crock Pot.
2. Add salt and pepper to taste and cover with a lid.
3. Cook on low settings for 8 hours.
4. Serve the chicken and veggies warm.

Ketchup Bean Stew

Servings: 6
Cooking Time: 4 1/4 Hours

Ingredients:
- 2 cans (15 oz. each) white beans, drained
- 1 tablespoon brown sugar
- 1 cup ketchup
- 1 teaspoon Dijon mustard
- 1/2 cup vegetable stock
- Salt and pepper to taste

Directions:
1. Combine all the ingredients in your Crock Pot.
2. Add salt and pepper to taste and cover. Cook on low settings for 4 hours.
3. Serve the stew warm and fresh.

Fajitas

Servings: 8
Cooking Time: 3 Hours

Ingredients:
- 1 and ½ pounds beef sirloin, cut into thin strips
- 2 tablespoons lemon juice
- 2 tablespoons olive oil
- 1 garlic clove, minced
- 1 and ½ teaspoon cumin, ground
- Salt and black pepper to the taste
- ½ teaspoon chili powder
- A pinch of red pepper flakes, crushed
- 1 red bell pepper, cut into thin strips
- 1 yellow onion, cut into thin strips
- 8 mini tortillas

Directions:
1. Heat up a pan with the oil over medium-high heat, add beef strips, brown them for a few minutes and transfer to your Crock Pot.
2. Add lemon juice, garlic, cumin, salt, pepper, chili powder and pepper flakes to the Crock Pot as well, cover and cook on High for 2 hours.
3. Add bell pepper and onion, stir and cook on High for 1 more hour.
4. Divide beef mix between your mini tortillas and serve for lunch.

Nutrition Info:
- calories 220, fat 9, fiber 2, carbs 14, protein 20

Red Cabbage Pork Stew

Servings: 6
Cooking Time: 4 1/4 Hours

Ingredients:
- 1 head red cabbage, shredded
- 1 1/2 pounds pork roast, cubed
- 2 tablespoons canola oil
- 1 large onion, chopped
- 4 garlic cloves, minced
- 1 tablespoon maple syrup
- 1 teaspoon chili powder
- 1/4 cup apple cider vinegar
- Salt and pepper to taste

Directions:
1. Combine all the ingredients in your crock pot.
2. Add salt and pepper to taste and cook the dish on low settings for 4 hours.
3. Serve the stew warm and fresh.

Buffalo Cauliflower

Servings: 6
Cooking Time: 6 1/4 Hours

Ingredients:
- 1 head cauliflower, cut into florets
- 1 onion, chopped
- 1 can diced tomatoes
- 1 can fire roasted green chilies, chopped
- 1 teaspoon hot sauce
- 1/2 cup tomato sauce
- 1 teaspoon cumin powder
- 1 can (15 oz.) cannellini beans, drained
- Salt and pepper to taste
- Grated Cheddar for serving

Directions:
1. Combine the cauliflower and the rest of the ingredients in your Crock Pot.
2. Add salt and pepper to taste and cook on low settings for 6 hours.
3. Serve the dish warm.

Carne Adovada

Servings: 6
Cooking Time: 6 Hours 20 Minutes

Ingredients:
- 12 hot New Mexico red chili pods
- 1 teaspoon ground cumin
- 3 cups chicken broth
- 2 garlic cloves, minced
- ½ teaspoon salt
- 1/8 cup canola oil
- 2 pounds boneless pork shoulder, chunked
- 1 teaspoon Mexican oregano

Directions:
1. Put canola oil and pork shoulder in a pan over medium heat and cook for about 2 minutes on each side.
2. Transfer to a crock pot and stir in the remaining ingredients.
3. Cover and cook on LOW for about 6 hours.
4. Dish out and serve hot.

Nutrition Info:
- Calories: 280 Fat: 10.6g Carbohydrates: 1.2g

Poultry Recipes

Poultry Recipes

Jalapeno Chicken Wings

Servings:6
Cooking Time: 3 Hours

Ingredients:
- 5 jalapenos, minced
- ½ cup tomato juice
- 2-pounds chicken wings, skinless
- 1 teaspoon salt
- ¼ cup of water

Directions:
1. Mix minced jalapenos with tomato juice, salt, and water.
2. Pour the liquid in the Crock Pot.
3. Add chicken wings and close the lid.
4. Cook the meal on High for 3 hours.

Nutrition Info:
- InfoPer Serving: 294 calories, 44.1g protein, 1.6g carbohydrates, 11.3g fat, 0.4g fiber, 135mg cholesterol, 573mg sodium, 439mg potassium.

Chicken Stuffed With Beans

Servings: 12
Cooking Time: 10 Hours

Ingredients:
- 21 oz. whole chicken
- 1 chili pepper, chopped
- 1 cup soybeans, canned
- 2 red onion, peeled and diced
- 1 carrot, peeled and diced
- 1 tsp onion powder
- 1 tsp cilantro, chopped
- 1 tsp oregano
- 1 tsp apple cider vinegar
- 1 tsp olive oil
- 1 tbsp dried basil
- 1 tsp paprika
- ¼ tsp ground red pepper
- ½ cup fresh dill
- 2 potatoes, peeled and diced
- 4 tbsp tomato sauce

Directions:

1. Blend chili pepper, onion powder, cilantro, oregano, olive oil, red pepper, tomato sauce, dill, paprika, basil, and vinegar in a blender.
2. Stuff the whole chicken with soybeans, and vegetables.
3. Brush it with the blender spice-chili mixture liberally.
4. Place the spiced chicken in the Crock Pot and pour the remaining spice mixture over it.
5. Put the cooker's lid on and set the cooking time to 10 hours on Low settings.
6. Slice and serve.

Nutrition Info:
- Per Serving: Calories: 186, Total Fat: 4.1g, Fiber: 5g, Total Carbs: 27.23g, Protein: 11g

Green Chili Chicken

Servings:6
Cooking Time: 8 Hours

Ingredients:
- 1 cup basil leaves
- ½ cup green chilies
- 2 tablespoon garlic salt
- 4 cloves of garlic
- 1 white onion, chopped
- 6 chicken thighs, bones and skin removed

Directions:
1. Place the basil, green chilies, garlic salt, garlic, and onion in a food processor. Pulse until smooth.
2. Place the chicken in the CrockPot and pour over the sauce.
3. Close the lid and cook on high for 6 hours or on low for 8 hours.

Nutrition Info:
- Calories per serving: 436; Carbohydrates: 2.6g; Protein: 32.3g; Fat: 32.1g; Sugar: 0g; Sodium: 988mg; Fiber: 1.4g

Harissa Chicken Breasts

Servings:6
Cooking Time: 8 Hours

Ingredients:
- 1 tablespoon olive oil
- 1-pound chicken breasts, skin and bones removed
- Salt to taste
- 2 tablespoon Harissa or Sriracha sauce
- 2 tablespoons toasted sesame seeds

Directions:
1. Pour oil in the crockpot.
2. Arrange the chicken breasts and season with salt and pepper to taste
3. Stir in the Sriracha or Harissa sauce. Give a good stir to incorporate everything.
4. Close the lid and cook on low for 8 hours or on high for 6 hours.
5. Once cooked, sprinkle toasted sesame seeds on top.

Nutrition Info:
- Calories per serving: 167; Carbohydrates: 1.1g; Protein: 16.3g; Fat: 10.6g; Sugar: 0g; Sodium: 632mg; Fiber: 0.6g

Chicken With Figs

Servings:4
Cooking Time: 7 Hours

Ingredients:
- 5 oz fresh figs, chopped
- 14 oz chicken fillet, chopped
- 1 cup of water
- 1 teaspoon peppercorns
- 1 tablespoon dried dill

Directions:
1. Put all ingredients in the Crock Pot.
2. Close the lid and cook the meal on Low for 7 hours.

Nutrition Info:
- InfoPer Serving: 280 calories, 30.1g protein, 23.4g carbohydrates, 7.7g fat, 3.7g fiber, 88mg cholesterol, 93mg sodium, 515mg potassium.

Thyme Whole Chicken

Servings:6
Cooking Time: 9 Hours

Ingredients:
- 1.5-pound whole chicken
- 1 tablespoon dried thyme
- 1 tablespoon olive oil
- 1 teaspoon salt
- 1 cup of water

Directions:
1. Chop the whole chicken roughly and sprinkle with dried thyme, olive oil, and salt.
2. Then transfer it in the Crock Pot, add water.
3. Cook the chicken on low for 9 hours.

Nutrition Info:
- InfoPer Serving: 237 calories, 32.9g protein, 0.3g carbohydrates, 10.8g fat, 0.2g fiber, 101mg cholesterol, 487mg sodium, 280mg potassium.

Easy Chicken Adobo

Servings:4
Cooking Time: 4 Hours

Ingredients:
- 1 teaspoon minced garlic
- 1 cup onion, chopped
- ½ teaspoon ground ginger
- 4 chicken thighs, skinless, boneless
- 1 tablespoon balsamic vinegar
- 1 tablespoon soy sauce
- ½ teaspoon ground black pepper
- ½ cup of water

Directions:
1. Put the onion in the Crock Pot.
2. Then mix soy sauce with balsamic vinegar and minced garlic.
3. Rub the chicken with garlic mixture and put it in the Crock Pot.
4. Then add ground black pepper, ginger, and water.
5. Cook the meal on High for 4 hours.

Nutrition Info:
- InfoPer Serving: 294 calories, 42.9g protein, 3.6g carbohydrates, 10.9g fat, 0.8g fiber, 130g cholesterol, 354mg sodium, 418mg potassium.

Chicken Wings And Mint Sauce

Servings: 6
Cooking Time: 4 Hours

Ingredients:
- 18 chicken wings, cut into halves
- 1 tablespoon turmeric
- 1 tablespoon cumin, ground
- 1 tablespoon ginger, grated
- 1 tablespoon coriander, ground
- 1 tablespoon paprika
- A pinch of cayenne pepper
- Salt and black pepper to the taste
- 2 tablespoons olive oil
- For the sauce:
- Juice of ½ lime
- 1 cup mint leaves
- 1 small ginger piece, chopped
- ¾ cup cilantro
- 1 tablespoon olive oil
- 1 tablespoon water
- Salt and black pepper to the taste
- 1 Serrano pepper

Directions:
1. In a bowl, mix 1 tablespoon ginger with cumin, coriander, paprika, turmeric, salt, pepper, cayenne and 2 tablespoons oil and stir well.
2. Add chicken wings pieces to this mix, toss to coat well and keep in the fridge for 20 minutes.
3. Add marinated wings to your Crock Pot, cook on High for 4 hours and transfer to a bowl.
4. In your blender, mix mint with cilantro, 1 small ginger pieces, juice of ½ lime, 1 tablespoon olive oil, salt, pepper, water and Serrano pepper and blend very well.
5. Serve your chicken wings with this sauce on the side.

Nutrition Info:
- calories 230, fat 5, fiber 1, carbs 12, protein 9

Peppercorn Chicken Thighs

Servings: 6
Cooking Time: 4 Hrs

Ingredients:
- 5 lbs. chicken thighs
- Salt and black pepper to the taste
- ½ cup white vinegar
- 1 tsp black peppercorns
- 4 garlic cloves, minced
- 3 bay leaves
- ½ cup of soy sauce

Directions:
1. Add chicken, peppercorns, and all other ingredients to the Crock Pot.
2. Put the cooker's lid on and set the cooking time to 4 hours on High settings.
3. Discard the bay leaves.
4. Serve warm.

Nutrition Info:
- Per Serving: Calories: 430, Total Fat: 12g, Fiber: 3g, Total Carbs: 10g, Protein: 36g

Maple Ginger Chicken

Servings: 4
Cooking Time: 15 Hours

Ingredients:
- ½ cup of soy sauce
- 1 tsp maple syrup
- 1 tbsp fresh ginger, grated
- 1 tsp salt
- 1 lb. chicken breast, diced
- 1 tsp ground ginger
- ¼ tsp ground cinnamon
- 2 tbsp red wine

Directions:
1. Toss chicken with maple syrup and all other ingredients in the Crock Pot.
2. Leave it for 10 minutes to marinate.
3. Put the cooker's lid on and set the cooking time to 15 hours on Low settings.
4. Serve warm.

Nutrition Info:
- Per Serving: Calories: 259, Total Fat: 13.5g, Fiber: 1g, Total Carbs: 6.71g, Protein: 26g

Sweet Chicken Mash

Servings:6
Cooking Time: 7 Hours

Ingredients:
- 3 tablespoons maple syrup
- 1-pound ground chicken
- 1 teaspoon dried dill
- 1 cup Cheddar cheese, shredded
- 1 cup of water

Directions:
1. Put all ingredients in the Crock Pot and carefully mix.
2. Close the lid and cook the mash on Low for 7 hours.

Nutrition Info:
- InfoPer Serving: 246 calories, 26.6g protein, 7g carbohydrates, 11.9g fat, 0g fiber, 87mg cholesterol, 184mg sodium, 229mg potassium.

Chicken With Basil And Tomatoes

Servings:4
Cooking Time: 8 Hours

Ingredients:
- ¾ cup balsamic vinegar
- ¼ cup fresh basil leaves
- 2 tablespoons olive oil
- 8 plum tomatoes, sliced
- 4 boneless chicken breasts, bone and skin removed

Directions:
1. Place balsamic vinegar, basil leaves, olive oil and tomatoes in a blender. Season with salt and pepper to taste. Pulse until fine.
2. Arrange the chicken pieces in the crockpot.
3. Pour over the sauce.
4. Close the lid and cook on low for 8 hours or on high for 6 hours.

Nutrition Info:
- Calories per serving: 177; Carbohydrates:4 g; Protein:24 g; Fat: 115g; Sugar: 0g; Sodium: 171mg; Fiber: 3.5g

Mushrooms Stuffed With Chicken

Servings: 6
Cooking Time: 3 Hours

Ingredients:
- 16 ounces button mushroom caps
- 4 ounces cream cheese
- ¼ cup carrot, chopped
- 1 teaspoon ranch seasoning mix
- 4 tablespoons hot sauce
- ¾ cup blue cheese, crumbled
- ¼ cup red onion, chopped
- ½ cup chicken meat, ground
- Salt and black pepper to the taste
- Cooking spray

Directions:
1. In a bowl, mix cream cheese with blue cheese, hot sauce, ranch seasoning, salt, pepper, chicken, carrot and red onion, stir and stuff mushrooms with this mix.
2. Grease your Crock Pot with cooking spray, add stuffed mushrooms, cover and cook on High for 3 hours.
3. Divide mushrooms between plates and serve.

Nutrition Info:
- calories 240, fat 4, fiber 1, carbs 12, protein 7

Turmeric Meatballs

Servings:4
Cooking Time: 2.5 Hours

Ingredients:
- 1-pound ground chicken
- 1 tablespoon ground turmeric
- ½ teaspoon ground ginger
- 1 teaspoon salt
- 1 tablespoon corn starch
- ½ cup cream

Directions:
1. Mix ground chicken with ground turmeric, ginger, salt, and corn starch.
2. Then make the medium-size meatballs.
3. Preheat the skillet well.
4. Put the meatballs in the hot skillet and cook them for 30 seconds per side.
5. Then transfer the meatballs in the Crock Pot, add cream, and close the lid.
6. Cook the meatballs on High for 2.5 hours.

Nutrition Info:
- InfoPer Serving: 250 calories, 33.2g protein, 4.5g carbohydrates, 10.3g fat, 0.4g fiber, 107mg cholesterol, 689mg sodium, 333mg potassium.

Cola Marinated Chicken

Servings: 6
Cooking Time: 5 Hours

Ingredients:
- 2 cup coca-cola
- 1 tbsp minced garlic
- 1 tsp salt
- 1 onion, wedged
- 16 oz. chicken, diced
- 1 tsp ground black pepper
- 1 tsp olive oil
- ½ cup fresh dill, chopped
- 2 tsp oregano

Directions:
1. Add coca-cola to a bowl and soak chicken for 15 minutes, then drain it.
2. Mix salt with garlic, olive oil, oregano, and black pepper in a small bowl.
3. Strain the chicken and reserve half of the coco-cola.
4. Transfer the chicken, coca-cola, and all other ingredients to the Crock Pot.
5. Put the cooker's lid on and set the cooking time to 5 hours on High settings.
6. Serve warm.

Nutrition Info:
- Per Serving: Calories: 154, Total Fat: 7g, Fiber: 1g, Total Carbs: 9.56g, Protein: 14g

Thai Chicken

Servings:4
Cooking Time: 4 Hours

Ingredients:
- 12 oz chicken fillet, sliced
- ½ cup of coconut milk
- 1 teaspoon dried lemongrass
- 1 teaspoon chili powder
- 1 teaspoon tomato paste
- 1 teaspoon ground cardamom
- 1 cup of water

Directions:
1. Rub the chicken with chili powder, tomato paste, ground cardamom, and dried lemongrass. Transfer it in the Crock Pot.
2. Add water and coconut milk.
3. Close the lid and cook the meal on High for 4 hours.

Nutrition Info:
- InfoPer Serving: 236 calories, 25.5g protein, 2.7g carbohydrates, 13.6g fat, 1.1g fiber, 76mg cholesterol, 87mg sodium, 321mg potassium.

Cyprus Chicken

Servings:4
Cooking Time: 4.5 Hours

Ingredients:
- 1-pound chicken breast, skinless, boneless
- 1 tablespoon sesame seeds
- ½ cup black olives, pitted and halved
- ½ cup pearl onions, peeled
- 1 teaspoon cumin seeds
- 1 cup of water

Directions:
1. Chop the chicken breast roughly and put it in the Crock Pot.
2. Add sesame seeds, black olives, onions, cumin seeds, and water.
3. Close the lid and cook the meal on high for 4.5 hours.

Nutrition Info:
- InfoPer Serving: 169 calories, 24.8g protein, 3.2g carbohydrates, 5.9g fat, 1.2g fiber, 73mg cholesterol, 208mg sodium, 463mg potassium.

Beef, Pork & Lamb Recipes

Beef, Pork & Lamb Recipes

Fall Pork

Servings:4
Cooking Time: 10 Hours

Ingredients:
- 9 oz pork tenderloin, chopped
- ½ cup carrot, chopped
- ½ cup pumpkin, chopped
- 2 cups of water
- 1 cup tomatoes, chopped
- 1 teaspoon Italian seasonings
- 1 teaspoon salt

Directions:
1. Put all ingredients in the Crock Pot.
2. Close the lid and cook the meal on Low for 10 hours.
3. Carefully mix the cooked meal before serving.

Nutrition Info:
- InfoPer Serving: 119 calories, 17.5g protein, 5.7g carbohydrates, 2.8g fat, 1.8g fiber, 47mg cholesterol, 635mg sodium, 484mg potassium

Oregano Pork Strips

Servings:4
Cooking Time: 7 Hours

Ingredients:
- 12 oz pork tenderloin, cut into strips
- 1 tablespoon dried oregano
- 1 cup of water
- 1 teaspoon salt

Directions:
1. Place pork strips in the Crock Pot.
2. Add all remaining ingredients and close the lid.
3. Cook the pork strips on Low for 7 hours.
4. Serve the cooked meal with hot gravy from the Crock Pot.

Nutrition Info:
- InfoPer Serving: 125 calories, 22.4g protein, 0.7g carbohydrates, 3.1g fat, 0.5g fiber, 62mg cholesterol, 632mg sodium, 378mg potassium

Beef Sausages In Maple Syrup

Servings:4
Cooking Time: 5 Hours

Ingredients:
- 1-pound beef sausages
- ½ cup maple syrup
- 3 tablespoons butter
- 1 teaspoon ground cumin
- ¼ cup of water

Directions:
1. Toss butter in the skillet and melt it.
2. Then pour the melted butter in the Crock Pot.
3. Add water, cumin, and maple syrup. Stir the liquid until smooth.
4. Add beef sausages and close the lid.
5. Cook the meal on High for 5 hours.

Nutrition Info:
- InfoPer Serving: 630 calories, 15.8 g protein, 29.7g carbohydrates, 50g fat, 0.1g fiber, 103mg cholesterol, 979mg sodium, 307mg potassium.

Ginger And Rosemary Pork Ribs

Servings:4
Cooking Time: 12 Hours

Ingredients:
- 1/3 cup chicken broth
- 4 racks pork spare ribs
- 3 tablespoons ginger paste or powder
- 1 tcaspoon roscmary, dricd
- Salt and pepper to taste

Directions:
1. Pour the broth into the crockpot.
2. Season the spare ribs with ginger paste, rosemary, salt and pepper.
3. Place in the crockpot.
4. Close the lid and cook on low for 12 hours or on high for 8 hours.

Nutrition Info:
- Calories per serving: 396; Carbohydrates: 03g; Protein: 27.1g; Fat: 21g; Sugar: 0g; Sodium: 582mg; Fiber: 0g

Saucy Beef Cheeks

Servings: 4
Cooking Time: 4 Hrs.

Ingredients:
- 4 beef cheeks, halved
- 2 tbsp olive oil
- Salt and black pepper to the taste
- 1 white onion, chopped
- 4 garlic cloves, minced
- 2 cup beef stock
- 5 cardamom pods
- 1 tbsp balsamic vinegar
- 3 bay leaves
- 7 cloves
- 2 vanilla beans, split
- 1 and ½ tbsp tomato paste
- 1 carrot, sliced

Directions:
1. Add beef cheeks and all remaining ingredients to the insert of your Crock Pot.
2. Put the cooker's lid on and set the cooking time to 4 hours on High settings.
3. Mix gently and serve warm.

Nutrition Info:
- Per Serving: Calories: 321, Total Fat: 5g, Fiber: 7g, Total Carbs: 18g, Protein: 12g

Beef Heart Saute

Servings:4
Cooking Time: 6 Hours

Ingredients:
- 1-pound beef heart, chopped
- 1 teaspoon fresh ginger, minced
- 2 tablespoons apple cider vinegar
- 1 sweet pepper, chopped
- 1 red onion, chopped
- 2 cups tomatoes
- 2 tablespoons sunflower oil
- 1 cup of water

Directions:
1. Heat the sunflower oil until hot in the skillet.
2. Add chopped beef heart and roast it for 10 minutes on medium heat.
3. Then transfer it in the Crock Pot.
4. Add all remaining ingredients and close the lid.
5. Cook the saute on low for 6 hours.

Nutrition Info:
- InfoPer Serving: 289 calories, 33.7g protein, 8.9g carbohydrates, 12.7g fat, 2.1g fiber, 240mg cholesterol, 75mg sodium, 570mg potassium.

Crockpot Cheeseburgers Casserole

Servings:4
Cooking Time: 8 Hours

Ingredients:
- 1 white onion, chopped
- 1 ½ pounds lean ground beef
- 2 tablespoons mustard
- 1 teaspoon dried basil leaves
- 2 cups cheddar cheese

Directions:
1. Heat skillet over medium flame and sauté both white onions and ground beef for 3 minutes. Continue stirring until lightly brown.
2. Transfer to the crockpot and stir in mustard and basil leaves. Season with salt and pepper.
3. Add cheese on top.
4. Close the lid and cook on low for 8 hours and on high for 6 hours.

Nutrition Info:
- Calories per serving: 472; Carbohydrates: 3g; Protein: 32.7g; Fat: 26.2g; Sugar: 0g; Sodium: 429mg; Fiber: 2.4g

Seasoned Poached Pork Belly

Servings:4
Cooking Time: 4 Hours

Ingredients:
- 10 oz pork belly
- 1 teaspoon minced garlic
- 1 teaspoon ginger paste
- ¼ cup apple cider vinegar
- 1 cup of water

Directions:
1. Rub the pork belly with minced garlic and garlic paste.
2. Then sprinkle it with apple cider vinegar and transfer in the Crock Pot.
3. Add water and close the lid.
4. Cook the pork belly on High for 4 hours.
5. Then slice the cooked pork belly and sprinkle with hot gravy from the Crock Pot.

Nutrition Info:
- InfoPer Serving: 333 calories, 32.8g protein, 0.7g carbohydrates, 19.1g fat, 0.1g fiber, 82mg cholesterol, 1148mg sodium, 20mg potassium

Barbacoa Beef

Servings:4
Cooking Time: 5 Hours

Ingredients:
- 1-pound beef chuck roast
- 1 teaspoon ground black pepper
- ½ teaspoon salt
- 1 teaspoon ground cumin
- ¼ lime,
- ½ teaspoon ground clove
- 2 cups of water

Directions:
1. Put the beef in the Crock Pot.
2. Add ground black pepper, salt, ground cumin, ground clove, and water.
3. Close the lid and cook the meat on High for 5 hours.
4. Then shred the beef.
5. Squeeze the line over the meat and carefully mix.

Nutrition Info:
- InfoPer Serving: 417 calories, 29.9g protein, 1.2g carbohydrates, 31.8g fat, 0.4g fiber, 117mg cholesterol, 369mg sodium, 283mg potassium.

Rosemary Pork

Servings: 4
Cooking Time: 7 Hours

Ingredients:
- 4 pork chops, bone in
- 1 cup chicken stock
- Salt and black pepper to the taste
- 1 teaspoon rosemary, dried
- 3 garlic cloves, minced

Directions:
1. Season pork chops with salt and pepper and place in your Crock Pot.
2. Add rosemary, garlic and stock, cover and cook on Low for 7 hours.
3. Divide pork between plates and drizzle cooking juices all over.

Nutrition Info:
- calories 165, fat 2, fiber 1, carbs 12, protein 26

Lamb Shoulder With Artichokes

Servings: 6
Cooking Time: 8 Hrs. 10 Minutes

Ingredients:
- 3 lbs. lamb shoulder, boneless
- 3 onions, roughly chopped
- 1 tbsp olive oil
- 1 tbsp oregano, chopped
- 6 garlic cloves, minced
- 1 tbsp lemon zest, grated
- Salt and black pepper to the taste
- ½ tsp allspice
- 1 and ½ cups veggie stock
- 14 oz. canned artichoke hearts, chopped
- ¼ cup tomato paste
- 2 tbsp parsley, chopped

Directions:
1. Place a suitable pan over medium-high heat and add oil.
2. Add lamb to the hot oil and cook for 5 minutes per side.
3. Transfer the lamb to the insert of the Crock Pot then stir in remaining ingredients except for the artichokes.
4. Put the cooker's lid on and set the cooking time to 8 hours on Low settings.
5. Stir in artichokes and cook for 15 minutes on low heat.
6. Serve warm.

Nutrition Info:
- Per Serving: Calories: 370, Total Fat: 4g, Fiber: 5g, Total Carbs: 12g, Protein: 16g

Cheesy Pork Casserole

Servings:4
Cooking Time: 10 Hours

Ingredients:
- 4 pork chops, bones removed and sliced
- 1 cauliflower head, cut into florets
- 1 cup chicken broth
- 1 teaspoon rosemary
- 2 cups cheddar cheese

Directions:
1. Arrange the pork chop slices in the crockpot,

2. Add in the cauliflower florets.
3. Pour the chicken broth and rosemary. Season with salt and pepper to taste.
4. Pour cheddar cheese on top.
5. Close the lid and cook on low for 10 hours.

Nutrition Info:
• Calories per serving: 417; Carbohydrates: 7g; Protein: 32.1g; Fat: 26.2g; Sugar: 0; Sodium: 846mg; Fiber: 5.3g

Pork Sweet Potato Stew

Servings: 6
Cooking Time: 4 Hrs.

Ingredients:
• 1 lb. sweet potatoes, chopped
• 3 and ½ lbs. pork roast
• 8 medium carrots, chopped
• Salt and black pepper to the taste
• 15 oz. canned tomatoes, chopped
• 1 yellow onion, chopped
• Grated zest and juice of 1 lemon
• 4 garlic cloves, minced
• 3 bay leaves
• Black pepper to the taste
• ½ cup kalamata olives pitted

Directions:
1. Add potatoes, carrots, and all other ingredients except the olives to the insert of the Crock Pot.
2. Put the cooker's lid on and set the cooking time to 4 hours on High settings.
3. Discard the bay leaves and transfer the meat to the serving plate.
4. Roughly mash the remaining veggies and add olives.
5. Transfer the veggies mix to the serving plate.
6. Serve warm.

Nutrition Info:
• Per Serving: Calories: 250, Total Fat: 4g, Fiber: 3g, Total Carbs: 6g, Protein: 13g

Meatballs In Vodka Sauce

Servings:4
Cooking Time: 6 Hours

Ingredients:
• 1-pound ground pork
• 1 onion, diced

• 1 teaspoon ground black pepper
• 1 tablespoon semolina
• 1 cup vodka sauce
• 2 tablespoons sesame oil

Directions:
1. In the mixing bowl mix ground pork with onion, ground black pepper, and semolina.
2. Make the small meatballs.
3. Brush the Crock Pot bottom with sesame oil and put the meatballs inside in one layer.
4. Add vodka sauce and close the lid.
5. Cook the meatballs on low for 6 hours.

Nutrition Info:
• InfoPer Serving: 299 calories, 32.9g protein, 10.3g carbohydrates, 13.4g fat, 0.8g fiber, 85mg cholesterol, 286mg sodium, 529mg potassium

Seasoned Beef Stew

Servings: 6
Cooking Time: 8 Hrs.

Ingredients:
• 4 lbs. beef roast
• 2 cups beef stock
• 2 sweet potatoes, cubed
• 6 carrots, sliced
• 7 celery stalks, chopped
• 1 yellow onion, chopped
• 1 tbsp onion powder
• 1 tbsp garlic powder
• 1 tbsp sweet paprika
• Salt and black pepper to the taste

Directions:
1. Add sweet potatoes, beef and all other ingredients to the insert of Crock Pot.
2. Put the cooker's lid on and set the cooking time to 8 hours on Low settings.
3. Slice the cooked roast and serve with mixed vegetables.
4. Enjoy.

Nutrition Info:
• Per Serving: Calories: 372, Total Fat: 6g, Fiber: 12g, Total Carbs: 19g, Protein: 11g

Parmesan Rosemary Potato

Servings: 5
Cooking Time: 4 Hrs

Ingredients:
- 1 lb. small potato, peeled
- ½ cup fresh dill, chopped
- 7 oz. Parmesan, shredded
- 1 tsp rosemary
- 1 tsp thyme
- 1 cup of water
- ¼ tsp chili flakes
- 3 tbsp cream
- 1 tsp salt

Directions:
1. Add potatoes, salt, rosemary, chili flakes, thyme, and water to the Crock Pot.
2. Put the cooker's lid on and set the cooking time to 2 hours on High settings.
3. Drizzle the remaining ingredients over the potatoes.
4. Cover again and slow cook for another 2 hours on High.
5. Serve warm.

Nutrition Info:
- Per Serving: Calories 235, Total Fat 3.9g, Fiber 2g, Total Carbs 32.26g, Protein 1g

Beef Roast With Cauliflower

Servings: 6
Cooking Time: 8 Hrs. 30 Minutes

Ingredients:
- 4 lbs. beef chuck roast
- 1 cup veggie stock
- 1 tbsp coconut oil
- 1 bay leaf
- 10 thyme sprigs
- 4 garlic cloves, minced
- 1 carrot, roughly chopped
- 1 yellow onion, roughly chopped
- 2 celery ribs, roughly chopped
- 1 cauliflower head, florets separated
- Salt and black pepper to the taste

Directions:
1. Place a suitable pan over medium-high heat and add oil to it.
2. Toss in the beef and drizzle salt and black pepper over it.
3. Sear the seasoned beef for 5 minutes per side then transfer to the insert of the Crock Pot.
4. Toss in the garlic, thyme springs, stock, bay leaf, celery, carrot, and onion.
5. Put the cooker's lid on and set the cooking time to 8 hours on Low settings.
6. Stir in cauliflower then cover again to cook for 20 minutes on High settings.
7. Serve warm.

Nutrition Info:
- Per Serving: Calories: 340, Total Fat: 5g, Fiber: 3g, Total Carbs: 14g, Protein: 22g

Fish & Seafood Recipes

Fish & Seafood Recipes

Shrimp With Spinach

Servings: 2
Cooking Time: 1 Hour

Ingredients:
- 1 pound shrimp, peeled and deveined
- 1 cup baby spinach
- ¼ cup tomato passata
- ½ cup chicken stock
- 3 scallions, chopped
- 1 tablespoon olive oil
- ½ teaspoon sweet paprika
- A pinch of salt and black pepper
- 1 tablespoon chives, chopped

Directions:
1. In your Crock Pot, mix the shrimp with the spinach, tomato passata and the other ingredients, toss, put the lid on and cook on High for 1 hour.
2. Divide the mix between plates and serve.

Nutrition Info:
- calories 200, fat 13, fiber 3, carbs 6, protein 11

Cilantro Salmon

Servings:4
Cooking Time: 3 Hours

Ingredients:
- 12 oz salmon fillet
- 1 teaspoon dried cilantro
- 1 tablespoon butter
- 1 teaspoon ground black pepper
- ½ cup of coconut milk

Directions:
1. Toss butter in the skillet and melt it.
2. Add salmon fillet and sprinkle it with ground black pepper. Roast the salmon on high heat for 1 minute per side.
3. Then put the fish in the Crock Pot.
4. Add coconut milk and cilantro.
5. Cook the fish on high for 3 hours.

Nutrition Info:
- InfoPer Serving: 208 calories, 17.3g protein, 2g carbohydrates, 15.3g fat, 0.8g fiber, 45mg cholesterol, 63mg sodium, 413mg potassium

Braised Salmon

Servings:4
Cooking Time: 1 Hour

Ingredients:
- 1 cup of water
- 2-pound salmon fillet
- 1 teaspoon salt
- 1 teaspoon ground black pepper

Directions:
1. Put all ingredients in the Crock Pot and close the lid.
2. Cook the salmon on High for 1 hour.

Nutrition Info:
- InfoPer Serving: 301 calories, 44.1g protein, 0.3g carbohydrates, 14g fat, 0.1g fiber, 100mg cholesterol, 683mg sodium, 878mg potassium.

Shrimp Clam Stew

Servings: 8
Cooking Time: 4 Hrs And 30 Minutes

Ingredients:
- 29 oz. canned tomatoes, chopped
- 2 yellow onions, chopped
- 2 celery ribs, chopped
- ½ cup fish stock
- 4 garlic cloves, minced
- 1 tbsp red vinegar
- 2 tbsp olive oil
- 3 lbs. shrimp, peeled and deveined
- 6 oz. canned clams
- 2 tbsp cilantro, chopped

Directions:
1. Add tomatoes, onion, vinegar, stock, celery, and oil to the Crock Pot.
2. Put the cooker's lid on and set the cooking time to 4 hours on Low settings.
3. Stir in cilantro, clams, and shrimp to the cooker.
4. Put the cooker's lid on and set the cooking time to 30 minutes on Low settings.

5. Serve warm.

Nutrition Info:
• Per Serving: Calories 255, Total Fat 4g, Fiber 3g, Total Carbs 14g, Protein 26g

Soy Sauce Scallops

Servings:4
Cooking Time: 30 Minutes

Ingredients:
• ¼ cup of soy sauce
• 1 tablespoon butter
• ½ teaspoon white pepper
• 1-pound scallops

Directions:
1. Pour soy sauce in the Crock Pot.
2. Add butter and white pepper.
3. After this, add scallops and close the lid.
4. Cook them on High for 30 minutes.

Nutrition Info:
• InfoPer Serving: 134 calories, 20.1g protein, 4.1g carbohydrates, 3.8g fat, 0.2g fiber, 45mg cholesterol, 1102mg sodium, 404mg potassium

Crockpot Shrimp Gambas

Servings:4
Cooking Time: 3 Hours

Ingredients:
• 1/3 cup extra virgin olive oil
• 5 cloves of garlic, chopped
• 1 teaspoon red pepper flakes
• 1 ¼ pounds shrimps, peeled and deveined
• 1 ¼ teaspoon Spanish paprika
• Salt and pepper to taste
• 2 tablespoons parsley, chopped

Directions:
1. Place all ingredients in the CrockPot.
2. Give a good stir.
3. Close the lid and cook on high for 2 hours or on low for 3 hours.

Nutrition Info:
• Calories per serving: 228; Carbohydrates: 3.8g; Protein: 29.8g; Fat: 12.6g; Sugar: 0g; Sodium: 633mg; Fiber: 2.1g

Crockpot Seafood Cioppino

Servings:8
Cooking Time: 4 Hours

Ingredients:
• 1-pound haddock fillets, cut into strips
• 1-pound shrimps, shelled and deveined
• 1 cup raw clam meat
• 1 cup crab meat
• 1 cup tomatoes, diced
• 2 onions, chopped
• 3 stalks of celery, chopped
• 2 cups clam juice
• 3 tablespoons tomato paste
• 5 cloves of garlic, minced
• 1 tablespoons olive oil
• 2 teaspoons Italian seasoning
• 1 bay leaf

Directions:
1. Place all ingredients in the CrockPot.
2. Give a good stir.
3. Close the lid and cook on high for 3 hours or on low for 4 hours.
4. Garnish with parsley.

Nutrition Info:
• Calories per serving: 217; Carbohydrates: 5.2g; Protein: 26.8g; Fat: 8.1g; Sugar: 0g; Sodium: 620mg; Fiber: 3.5g

Paprika Shrimp

Servings: 3
Cooking Time: 4 Hours 20 Minutes

Ingredients:
• 1 pound tiger shrimp
• Salt, to taste
• ½ teaspoon smoked paprika
• 2 tablespoons tea seed oil

Directions:
1. Mix together all the ingredients in a large bowl until well combined.
2. Transfer the shrimp in the crock pot and cover the lid.
3. Cook on LOW for about 4 hours and dish out to serve with roasted tomatoes and jalapenos.

Nutrition Info:
• Calories: 231 Fat: 10.4g Carbohydrates: 0.2g

Moroccan Fish

Servings: 9
Cooking Time: 3 Hours 20 Minutes

Ingredients:
- 1 pound cherry tomatoes, crushed slightly
- 1 teaspoon tea seed oil
- 1 teaspoon red pepper flakes, crushed
- 3 pounds salmon fillets
- 2 garlic cloves, crushed
- Salt, to taste
- 1 tablespoon fresh basil leaves, torn
- 1 teaspoon dried oregano, crushed

Directions:
1. Put the tea seed oil and salmon fillets in the crock pot and cover the lid.
2. Cook on LOW for about 2 hours and add cherry tomatoes, garlic, oregano, salt and red pepper flakes.
3. Cook on HIGH for about 1 hour and garnish with basil leaves to serve.

Nutrition Info:
- Calories: 243 Fat: 11.3g Carbohydrates: 2.7g

Tender Tilapia In Cream Sauce

Servings:4
Cooking Time: 5 Hours

Ingredients:
- 4 tilapia fillets
- ½ cup heavy cream
- 1 teaspoon garlic powder
- 1 teaspoon ground black pepper
- ½ teaspoon salt
- 1 teaspoon cornflour

Directions:
1. Mix cornflour with cream until smooth.
2. Then pour the liquid in the Crock Pot.
3. After this, sprinkle the tilapia fillets with garlic powder, ground black pepper, and salt.
4. Place the fish fillets in the Crock Pot and close the lid.
5. Cook the fish on Low for 5 hours.

Nutrition Info:
- InfoPer Serving: 151 calories, 21.6g protein, 1.7g carbohydrates, 6.6g fat, 0.3g fiber, 76mg cholesterol, 337mg sodium, 28mg potassium

Garlic Tuna

Servings:4
Cooking Time: 2 Hours

Ingredients:
- 1-pound tuna fillet
- 1 teaspoon garlic powder
- 1 tablespoon olive oil
- ½ cup of water

Directions:
1. Sprinkle the tuna fillet with garlic powder.
2. Then pour olive oil in the skillet and heat it well.
3. Add the tuna and roast it for 1 minute per side.
4. Transfer the tuna in the Crock Pot.
5. Add water and cook it on High for 2 hours.

Nutrition Info:
- InfoPer Serving: 444 calories, 23.9g protein, 0.5g carbohydrates, 38.7g fat, 0.1g fiber, 0mg cholesterol, 1mg sodium, 8mg potassium

Trout Capers Piccata

Servings: 4
Cooking Time: 45 Minutes

Ingredients:
- 4 oz dry white wine
- 1 lb. trout fillet
- 2 tbsp capers
- 3 tbsp olive oil
- 3 tbsp flour
- 1 tsp garlic powder
- 1 tsp dried rosemary
- 1 tsp oregano
- 1 tsp cilantro
- 1 tbsp fresh dill, chopped
- 1 tsp ground white pepper
- 1 tsp butter

Directions:
1. Pour olive oil into the insert of Crock Pot then place the trout in it.
2. Add garlic powder, dried rosemary, white pepper, cilantro, and oregano over the trout.
3. Put the cooker's lid on and set the cooking time to 30 minutes on High settings.
4. Flip the fish when cooked halfway through.
5. Meanwhile, mix dry wine with flour and add to the cooker.
6. Add butter, capers, and dill on top.

7. Put the cooker's lid on and set the cooking time to 15 minutes on High settings.
8. Serve warm.

Nutrition Info:
• Per Serving: Calories: 393, Total Fat: 25.9g, Fiber: 1g, Total Carbs: 8g, Protein: 32g

Mozzarella Fish Casserole

Servings:4
Cooking Time: 2.5 Hours

Ingredients:
• 1 cup Mozzarella, shredded
• 1-pound salmon fillet, chopped
• 1 cup onion, sliced
• 1 teaspoon salt
• ½ cup of water
• 1 teaspoon avocado oil

Directions:
1. Mix salmon with salt and put it in the Crock Pot.
2. Add avocado oil and water.
3. After this, top the fish with sliced onion and Mozzarella.
4. Close the lid and cook the casserole on High for 2.5 hours.

Nutrition Info:
• InfoPer Serving: 183 calories, 24.3g protein, 3g carbohydrates, 8.4g fat, 0.7g fiber, 54mg cholesterol, 676mg sodium, 482mg potassium

Vegan Milk Clams

Servings:4
Cooking Time: 3 Hours

Ingredients:
• 1 cup organic almond milk
• 1 teaspoon dried parsley
• 1 teaspoon dried dill
• ½ teaspoon salt
• 1-pound clams

Directions:
1. Put all ingredients in the Crock Pot and gently mix.
2. Close the lid and cook the clams on Low for 3 hours.

Nutrition Info:
• InfoPer Serving: 70 calories, 1g protein, 14.6g carbohydrates, 0.9g fat, 0.5g fiber, 0mg cholesterol, 737mg sodium, 111mg potassium

Chili Bigeye Jack (tuna)

Servings:4
Cooking Time: 3.5 Hours

Ingredients:
• 9 oz tuna fillet (bigeye jack), roughly chopped
• 1 teaspoon chili powder
• 1 teaspoon curry paste
• ½ cup of coconut milk
• 1 tablespoon sesame oil

Directions:
1. Mix curry paste and coconut milk and pour the liquid in the Crock Pot.
2. Add tuna fillet and sesame oil.
3. Then add chili powder.
4. Cook the meal on High for 3.5 hours.

Nutrition Info:
• InfoPer Serving: 341 calories, 14.2g protein, 2.4g carbohydrates, 31.2g fat, 0.9g fiber, 0mg cholesterol, 11mg sodium, 91mg potassium

Curry Squid

Servings:5
Cooking Time: 3 Hours

Ingredients:
• 15 oz squid, peeled, sliced
• 1 teaspoon curry paste
• ½ cup of coconut milk
• ¼ cup of water
• 1 teaspoon dried dill
• 1 teaspoon ground nutmeg

Directions:
1. Mix coconut milk with water and curry paste.
2. Then pour the liquid in the Crock Pot.
3. Add dried dill and ground nutmeg.
4. After this, add the sliced squid and close the lid.
5. Cook the meal on low for 3 hours.

Nutrition Info:
• InfoPer Serving: 143 calories, 13.9g protein, 4.6g carbohydrates, 7.6g fat, 0.7g fiber, 198mg cholesterol, 42mg sodium, 281mg potassium.

Vegetable & Vegetarian Recipes

Vegetable & Vegetarian Recipes

Vegetarian Keto Burgers

Servings:4
Cooking Time: 4 Hours

Ingredients:
- 2 Portobello mushrooms, chopped
- 2 tablespoons basil, chopped
- 1 clove of garlic, minced
- 1 egg, beaten
- ½ cup boiled cauliflower, mashed

Directions:
1. Line the bottom of the crockpot with foil.
2. In a food processor, combine all ingredients.
3. Make 4 burger patties using your hands and place gently in the crockpot.
4. Close the lid and cook on low for 4 hours or on high for 3 hours.

Nutrition Info:
- Calories per serving: 134; Carbohydrates: 18g; Protein: 10g; Fat: 3.1g; Sugar:0.9g; Sodium:235mg; Fiber: 5g

Quinoa Casserole

Servings:6
Cooking Time: 3 Hours

Ingredients:
- 1 teaspoon nutritional yeast
- 1 cup quinoa
- 1 cup bell pepper, chopped
- 1 teaspoon smoked paprika
- 1 cup broccoli florets, chopped
- 1 cup cashew cream
- 1 teaspoon chili flakes
- 3 cups of water

Directions:
1. Mix quinoa with nutritional yeast and put in the Crock Pot.
2. Add bell pepper, smoked paprika, broccoli florets, and chili flakes.
3. Add cashew cream and water.
4. Close the lid and cook the casserole for 3 hours on high.

Nutrition Info:
- InfoPer Serving: 121 calories, 4.9g protein, 23.1g carbohydrates, 2.1g fat, 2.9g fiber, 0mg cholesterol, 13mg sodium, 268mg potassium.

Tofu Curry

Servings:4
Cooking Time: 3 Hours

Ingredients:
- 1 cup chickpeas, cooked
- 8 oz firm tofu, chopped
- 1 teaspoon curry powder
- ½ cup of coconut milk
- 1 teaspoon ground coriander
- 1 cup vegetable stock
- 1 red onion, diced

Directions:
1. In the mixing bowl mix curry powder, coconut milk, ground coriander, and red onion.
2. Mix the curry mixture with tofu.
3. Then pour the vegetable stock in the Crock Pot.
4. Add chickpeas, tofu, and all remaining curry mixture.
5. Close the lid and cook the meal on Low for 3 hours. Don't stir the cooked meal.

Nutrition Info:
- InfoPer Serving: 306 calories, 15.3g protein, 36.3g carbohydrates, 13.1g fat, 10.6g fiber, 0mg cholesterol, 205mg sodium, 649mg potassium.

Tomato Okra

Servings:2
Cooking Time: 6 Hours

Ingredients:
- 2 cups okra, sliced
- 1 teaspoon chili powder
- 1 teaspoon salt
- 1 cup tomato juice
- ¼ cup fresh parsley, chopped

Directions:
1. Put all ingredients in the Crock Pot and carefully

mix.
2. Close the lid and cook the okra on Low for 6 hours.

Nutrition Info:
• InfoPer Serving: 67 calories, 3.2g protein, 13.8g carbohydrates, 0.5g fat, 4.4g fiber, 0mg cholesterol, 1514mg sodium, 644mg potassium.

Garlic Asparagus

Servings:5
Cooking Time: 6 Hours

Ingredients:
• 1-pound asparagus, trimmed
• 1 teaspoon salt
• 1 teaspoon garlic powder
• 1 tablespoon vegan butter
• 1 ½ cup vegetable stock

Directions:
1. Chop the asparagus roughly and sprinkle with salt and garlic powder.
2. Put the vegetables in the Crock Pot.
3. Add vegan butter and vegetable stock. Close the lid.
4. Cook the asparagus on Low for 6 hours.

Nutrition Info:
• InfoPer Serving: 33 calories, 2.3g protein, 6.1g carbohydrates, 1g fat, 2g fiber, 0mg cholesterol, 687mg sodium, 190mg potassium.

Cheddar Mushrooms

Servings:4
Cooking Time: 6 Hours

Ingredients:
• 4 cups cremini mushrooms, sliced
• 1 teaspoon dried oregano
• 1 teaspoon ground black pepper
• ½ teaspoon salt
• 1 cup Cheddar cheese, shredded
• 1 cup heavy cream
• 1 cup of water

Directions:
1. Pour water and heavy cream in the Crock Pot.
2. Add salt, ground black pepper, and dried oregano.
3. Then add sliced mushrooms, and Cheddar cheese.
4. Cook the meal on Low for 6 hours.
5. When the mushrooms are cooked, gently stir them and transfer in the serving plates.

Nutrition Info:
• InfoPer Serving: 239 calories, 9.6g protein, 4.8g carbohydrates, 20.6g fat, 0.7g fiber, 71mg cholesterol, 484mg sodium, 386mg potassium.

Okra Curry

Servings:4
Cooking Time: 2.5 Hours

Ingredients:
• 1 cup potatoes, chopped
• 1 cup okra, chopped
• 1 cup tomatoes, chopped
• 1 teaspoon curry powder
• 1 teaspoon dried dill
• 1 cup coconut cream
• 1 cup of water

Directions:
1. Pour water in the Crock Pot.
2. Add coconut cream, potatoes, tomatoes, curry powder, and dried dill.
3. Cook the ingredients on High for 2 hours.
4. Then add okra and carefully mix the meal.
5. Cook it for 30 minutes on High.

Nutrition Info:
• InfoPer Serving: 184 calories, 3g protein, 13.3g carbohydrates, 14.6g fat, 3.8g fiber, 0mg cholesterol, 18mg sodium, 508mg potassium.

Zucchini Basil Soup

Servings:8
Cooking Time: 3 Hours

Ingredients:
• 9 cups zucchini, diced
• 2 cups white onions, chopped
• 4 cups vegetable broth
• 8 cloves of garlic, minced
• 1 cup basil leaves
• 4 tablespoons olive oil
• Salt and pepper to taste

Directions:
1. Place the ingredients in the CrockPot.
2. Give a good stir.
3. Close the lid and cook on high for 2 hours or on low for 3 hours.
4. Once cooked, transfer into a blender and pulse until smooth.

Nutrition Info:
- Calories per serving: 93; Carbohydrates: 5.4g; Protein: 1.3g; Fat: 11.6g; Sugar: 0g; Sodium: 322mg; Fiber: 4.2g

Hot Sauce Oysters Mushrooms

Servings:4
Cooking Time: 2 Hours

Ingredients:
- 2 tablespoons hot sauce
- 2 cups oysters mushrooms, sliced
- ½ cup of water
- 1 tablespoon avocado oil
- 1 teaspoon dried dill
- 1 teaspoon salt

Directions:
1. Mix sliced oysters with avocado oil, dried dill, and salt.
2. Put them in the Crock Pot.
3. Add water and cook the mushrooms on High for 2 hours.
4. After this, drain the mushrooms and mix them with hot sauce.

Nutrition Info:
- InfoPer Serving: 15 calories, 1.1g protein, 2.2g carbohydrates, 0.6g fat, 0.9g fiber, 0mg cholesterol, 778mg sodium, 149mg potassium.

Couscous Halloumi Salad

Servings: 5
Cooking Time: 4 Hrs

Ingredients:
- 1 cup couscous
- 1 green sweet pepper, chopped
- 2 garlic cloves
- 1 cup beef broth
- 1 tsp chives
- ½ cup cherry tomatoes halved
- 1 zucchini, diced
- 7 oz. halloumi cheese, chop
- 1 tsp olive oil
- 1 tsp paprika
- ¼ tsp ground cardamom
- 1 tsp salt

Directions:
1. Add couscous, cardamom, salt, and paprika to the Crock Pot.
2. Stir in garlic, zucchini, and beef broth to the couscous.
3. Put the cooker's lid on and set the cooking time to 4 hours on High settings.
4. Stir in the remaining ingredients and toss it gently.
5. Serve.

Nutrition Info:
- Per Serving: Calories 170, Total Fat 9.6g, Fiber 1g, Total Carbs 12.59g, Protein 9g

Rainbow Bake

Servings:4
Cooking Time: 6 Hours

Ingredients:
- 1 zucchini, sliced
- 1 tomato, sliced
- 1 eggplant, sliced
- 1 red onion, sliced
- 1 tablespoon coconut oil
- 1 teaspoon salt
- 1 teaspoon dried parsley
- 1 teaspoon chili powder
- 1 cup of water

Directions:
1. Carefully grease the Crock Pot bowl with coconut oil.
2. Then put zucchini, tomato, eggplant, and onion in the Crock Pot one-by-one.
3. Sprinkle the vegetables with salt, dried parsley, and chili powder.
4. Add water and close the lid.
5. Cook the meal on Low for 6 hours.

Nutrition Info:
- InfoPer Serving: 82 calories, 2.2g protein, 11.9g carbohydrates, 3.9g fat, 5.6g fiber, 0mg cholesterol, 597mg sodium, 482mg potassium.

Mushroom Bourguignon

Servings:3
Cooking Time: 7 Hours

Ingredients:
- ½ cup mushrooms, chopped
- ¼ cup onion, chopped
- ¼ cup carrot, diced
- ½ cup green peas, frozen
- 1 teaspoon dried thyme
- 1 teaspoon salt
- 2 tablespoons tomato paste
- 3 cups vegetable stock

Directions:
1. Mix vegetable stock with tomato paste and pour liquid in the Crock Pot.
2. Add all remaining ingredients and close the lid.
3. Cook the meal on Low for 7 hours.

Nutrition Info:
- InfoPer Serving: 45 calories, 2.8g protein, 8.8g carbohydrates, 0.3g fat, 2.9g fiber, 0mg cholesterol, 844mg sodium, 250mg potassium.

Mushroom Steaks

Servings:4
Cooking Time: 2 Hours

Ingredients:
- 4 Portobello mushrooms
- 1 tablespoon avocado oil
- 1 tablespoon lemon juice
- 2 tablespoons coconut cream
- ½ teaspoon ground black pepper

Directions:
1. Slice Portobello mushrooms into steaks and sprinkle with avocado oil, lemon juice, coconut cream, and ground black pepper.
2. Then arrange the mushroom steaks in the Crock Pot in one layer (you will need to cook all mushroom steaks by 2 times).
3. Cook the meal on High for 1 hour.

Nutrition Info:
- InfoPer Serving: 43 calories, 3.3g protein, 3.9g carbohydrates, 2.3g fat, 1.4g fiber, 0mg cholesterol, 2mg sodium, 339mg potassium.

Yam Fritters

Servings:1
Cooking Time: 4 Hours

Ingredients:
- 1 yam, grated, boiled
- 1 teaspoon dried parsley
- ¼ teaspoon chili powder
- ¼ teaspoon salt
- 1 egg, beaten
- 1 teaspoon flour
- 5 tablespoons coconut cream
- Cooking spray

Directions:
1. In the mixing bowl mix grated yams, dried parsley, chili powder, salt, egg, and flour.
2. Make the fritters from the yam mixture.
3. After this, spray the Crock Pot bottom with cooking spray.
4. Put the fritters inside in one layer.
5. Add coconut cream and cook the meal on Low for 4 hours.

Nutrition Info:
- InfoPer Serving: 115 calories, 6.4g protein, 4.9g carbohydrates, 7.9g fat, 0.4g fiber, 175mg cholesterol, 670mg sodium, 110mg potassium.

Arugula And Halloumi Salad

Servings:4
Cooking Time: 30 Minutes

Ingredients:
- 1 tablespoon coconut oil
- 1 teaspoon smoked paprika
- ½ teaspoon ground turmeric
- ½ teaspoon garlic powder
- 2 cups arugula, chopped
- 1 cup cherry tomatoes
- 1 tablespoon olive oil
- 6 oz halloumi

Directions:
1. Slice the halloumi and sprinkle with melted coconut oil.
2. Put the cheese in the Crock Pot in one layer and cook on high for 15 minutes per side.
3. Meanwhile, mix arugula with cherry tomatoes in the salad bowl.
4. Add cooked halloumi, smoked paprika, ground tur-

meric, garlic powder, and olive oil.
5. Shake the salad gently.

Nutrition Info:
• InfoPer Serving: 210 calories, 9.9g protein, 4.4g carbohydrates, 17.8g fat, 1g fiber, 29mg cholesterol, 430mg sodium, 167mg potassium.

Swedish Style Beets

Servings:4
Cooking Time: 8 Hours

Ingredients:
• 1-pound beets
• ¼ cup apple cider vinegar
• 1 tablespoon olive oil
• 1 teaspoon salt
• ½ teaspoon sugar
• 3 cups of water

Directions:
1. Put beets in the Crock Pot.
2. Add water and cook the vegetables for 8 hours on Low.
3. Then drain water and peel the beets.
4. Chop the beets roughly and put in the big bowl.
5. Add all remaining ingredients and leave the beets for 2-3 hours to marinate.

Nutrition Info:
• InfoPer Serving: 85 calories, 1.9g protein, 11.9g carbohydrates, 3.7g fat, 2.3g fiber, 0mg cholesterol, 675mg sodium, 359mg potassium.

Vegetable Bean Stew

Servings: 8
Cooking Time: 7 Hrs

Ingredients:
• ½ cup barley
• 1 cup black beans
• ¼ cup red beans
• 2 carrots, peeled and julienned
• 1 cup onion, chopped
• 1 cup tomato juice
• 2 potatoes, peeled and diced
• 1 tsp salt
• 1 tsp ground black pepper
• 4 cups of water
• 4 oz. tofu
• 1 tsp garlic powder

• 1 cup fresh cilantro

Directions:
1. Add black beans, red beans, and barley to the Crock Pot.
2. Stir in tomato juice, onion, garlic powder, black pepper, salt, and water.
3. Put the cooker's lid on and set the cooking time to 4 hours on High settings.
4. Add carrots, cilantro, and potatoes to the cooker.
5. Put the cooker's lid on and set the cooking time to 3 hours on Low settings.
6. Serve warm.

Nutrition Info:
• Per Serving: Calories 207, Total Fat 3.5g, Fiber 8g, Total Carbs 37.67g, Protein 8g

Side Dish Recipes

Side Dish Recipes

Thyme Mushrooms And Corn

Servings: 2
Cooking Time: 4 Hours

Ingredients:
- 4 garlic cloves, minced
- 1 tablespoon olive oil
- 1 pound white mushroom caps, halved
- 1 cup corn
- 1 cup canned tomatoes, crushed
- ¼ teaspoon thyme, dried
- ½ cup veggie stock
- A pinch of salt and black pepper
- 2 tablespoons parsley, chopped

Directions:
1. Grease your Crock Pot with the oil, and mix the garlic with the mushrooms, corn and the other ingredients inside.
2. Toss, put the lid on and cook on Low for 4 hours.
3. Divide between plates and serve as a side dish.

Nutrition Info:
- calories 122, fat 6, fiber 1, carbs 8, protein 5

Asian Sesame Asparagus

Servings: 4
Cooking Time: 4 Hrs.

Ingredients:
- 1 tbsp sesame seeds
- 1 tsp miso paste
- ¼ cup of soy sauce
- 1 cup fish stock
- 8 oz. asparagus
- 1 tsp salt
- 1 tsp chili flakes
- 1 tsp oregano
- 1 cup of water

Directions:
1. Fill the insert of the Crock Pot with water and add asparagus.
2. Put the cooker's lid on and set the cooking time to 3 hours on High settings.
3. During this time, mix miso paste with soy sauce, fish stock, and sesame seeds in a suitable bowl.
4. Stir in oregano, chili flakes, and salt, then mix well.
5. Drain the slow-cooked asparagus then return it to the Crock Pot.
6. Pour the miso-stock mixture over the asparagus.
7. Put the cooker's lid on and set the cooking time to 1 hour on High settings.
8. Serve warm.

Nutrition Info:
- Per Serving: Calories: 85, Total Fat: 4.8g, Fiber: 2g, Total Carbs: 7.28g, Protein: 4g

Chicken With Sweet Potato

Servings: 6
Cooking Time: 3 Hours

Ingredients:
- 16 oz. sweet potato, peeled and diced
- 3 cups chicken stock
- 1 tbsp salt
- 3 tbsp margarine
- 2 tbsp cream cheese

Directions:
1. Add sweet potato, chicken stock, and salt to the Crock Pot.
2. Put the cooker's lid on and set the cooking time to 5 hours on High settings.
3. Drain the slow-cooked potatoes and transfer them to a suitable bowl.
4. Mash the sweet potatoes and stir in cream cheese and margarine.
5. Serve fresh.

Nutrition Info:
- Per Serving: Calories: 472, Total Fat: 31.9g, Fiber: 6.7g, Total Carbs: 43.55g, Protein: 3g

Stewed Okra

Servings: 4
Cooking Time: 3 Hours

Ingredients:
- 2 cups okra, sliced
- 2 garlic cloves, minced
- 6 ounces tomato sauce
- 1 red onion, chopped
- A pinch of cayenne peppers
- 1 teaspoon liquid smoke
- Salt and black pepper to the taste

Directions:
1. In your Crock Pot, mix okra with garlic, onion, cayenne, tomato sauce, liquid smoke, salt and pepper, cover, cook on Low for 3 hours.
2. Divide between plates and serve as a side dish.

Nutrition Info:
- calories 182, fat 3, fiber 6, carbs 8, protein 3

Garlic Carrots Mix

Servings: 2
Cooking Time: 4 Hours

Ingredients:
- 1 pound carrots, sliced
- 2 garlic cloves, minced
- 1 red onion, chopped
- 1 tablespoon olive oil
- ½ cup tomato sauce
- A pinch of salt and black pepper
- ½ teaspoon oregano, dried
- 2 teaspoons lemon zest, grated
- 1 tablespoon lemon juice
- 1 tablespoon chives, chopped

Directions:
1. In your Crock Pot, mix the carrots with the garlic, onion and the other ingredients, toss, put the lid on and cook on Low for 4 hours.
2. Divide the mix between plates and serve.

Nutrition Info:
- calories 219, fat 8, fiber 4, carbs 8, protein 17

Italian Squash And Peppers Mix

Servings: 4
Cooking Time: 1 Hour And 30 Minutes

Ingredients:
- 12 small squash, peeled and cut into wedges
- 2 red bell peppers, cut into wedges
- 2 green bell peppers, cut into wedges
- 1/3 cup Italian dressing
- 1 red onion, cut into wedges
- Salt and black pepper to the taste
- 1 tablespoon parsley, chopped

Directions:
1. In your Crock Pot, mix squash with red bell peppers, green bell peppers, salt, pepper and Italian dressing, cover and cook on High for 1 hour and 30 minutes.
2. Add parsley, toss, divide between plates and serve as a side dish.

Nutrition Info:
- calories 80, fat 2, fiber 3, carbs 11, protein 2

Cauliflower Rice And Spinach

Servings: 8
Cooking Time: 3 Hours

Ingredients:
- 2 garlic cloves, minced
- 2 tablespoons butter, melted
- 1 yellow onion, chopped
- ¼ teaspoon thyme, dried
- 3 cups veggie stock
- 20 ounces spinach, chopped
- 6 ounces coconut cream
- Salt and black pepper to the taste
- 2 cups cauliflower rice

Directions:
1. Heat up a pan with the butter over medium heat, add onion, stir and cook for 4 minutes.
2. Add garlic, thyme and stock, stir, cook for 1 minute more and transfer to your Crock Pot.
3. Add spinach, coconut cream, cauliflower rice, salt and pepper, stir a bit, cover and cook on High for 3 hours.
4. Divide between plates and serve as a side dish.

Nutrition Info:
- calories 200, fat 4, fiber 4, carbs 8, protein 2

Chorizo And Cauliflower Mix

Servings: 4
Cooking Time: 5 Hours

Ingredients:
- 1 pound chorizo, chopped
- 12 ounces canned green chilies, chopped
- 1 yellow onion, chopped
- ½ teaspoon garlic powder
- Salt and black pepper to the taste
- 1 cauliflower head, riced
- 2 tablespoons green onions, chopped

Directions:
1. Heat up a pan over medium heat, add chorizo and onion, stir, brown for a few minutes and transfer to your Crock Pot.
2. Add chilies, garlic powder, salt, pepper, cauliflower and green onions, toss, cover and cook on Low for 5 hours.
3. Divide between plates and serve as a side dish.

Nutrition Info:
- calories 350, fat 12, fiber 4, carbs 6, protein 20

Dill Mixed Fennel

Servings: 7
Cooking Time: 3 Hour

Ingredients:
- 10 oz. fennel bulbs, diced
- 2 tbsp olive oil
- 1 tsp ground black pepper
- 1 tsp paprika
- 1 tsp cilantro
- 1 tsp oregano
- 1 tsp basil
- 3 tbsp white wine
- 1 tsp salt
- 2 garlic cloves
- 1 tsp dried dill

Directions:
1. Add fennel bulbs and all other ingredients to the Crock Pot.
2. Put the cooker's lid on and set the cooking time to 3.5 hours on High settings.
3. Serve warm.

Nutrition Info:
- Per Serving: Calories: 53, Total Fat: 4.1g, Fiber: 2g, Total Carbs: 4g, Protein: 1g

Green Beans With Mushrooms

Servings: 4
Cooking Time: 3 Hours

Ingredients:
- 1 lb. fresh green beans, trimmed
- 1 small yellow onion, chopped
- 6 oz. bacon, chopped
- 1 garlic clove, minced
- 1 cup chicken stock
- 8 oz. mushrooms, sliced
- Salt and black pepper to the taste
- A splash of balsamic vinegar

Directions:
1. Add green beans, onion, stock and rest of the ingredients to the Crock Pot.
2. Put the cooker's lid on and set the cooking time to 3 hours on Low settings.
3. Serve warm.

Nutrition Info:
- Per Serving: Calories: 162, Total Fat: 4g, Fiber: 5g, Total Carbs: 8g, Protein: 4g

Beans And Red Peppers

Servings: 2
Cooking Time: 2 Hrs.

Ingredients:
- 2 cups green beans, halved
- 1 red bell pepper, cut into strips
- Salt and black pepper to the taste
- 1 tbsp olive oil
- 1 and ½ tbsp honey mustard

Directions:
1. Add green beans, honey mustard, red bell pepper, oil, salt, and black to Crock Pot.
2. Put the cooker's lid on and set the cooking time to 2 hours on High settings.
3. Serve warm.

Nutrition Info:
- Per Serving: Calories: 50, Total Fat: 0g, Fiber: 4g, Total Carbs: 8g, Protein: 2g

Tomato And Corn Mix

Servings: 2
Cooking Time: 4 Hours

Ingredients:
- 1 red onion, sliced
- 2 spring onions, chopped
- 1 cup corn
- 1 cup tomatoes, cubed
- 1 tablespoon olive oil
- ½ red bell pepper, chopped
- ½ cup tomato sauce
- ¼ teaspoon sweet paprika
- ½ teaspoon cumin, ground
- 1 tablespoon chives, chopped
- Salt and black pepper to the taste

Directions:
1. Heat up a pan with the oil over medium-high heat, add the onion , spring onions and bell pepper and cook for 10 minutes.
2. Transfer the mix to the Crock Pot, add the corn and the other ingredients, toss, put the lid on and cook on Low for 4 hours.
3. Divide the mix between plates and serve as a side dish.

Nutrition Info:
- calories 312, fat 4, fiber 6, carbs 12, protein 6

Hot Lentils

Servings: 2
Cooking Time: 6 Hours

Ingredients:
- 1 tablespoon thyme, chopped
- ½ tablespoon olive oil
- 1 cup canned lentils, drained
- ½ cup veggie stock
- 2 garlic cloves, minced
- 1 tablespoon cider vinegar
- 2 tablespoons tomato paste
- 1 tablespoon rosemary, chopped

Directions:
1. In your Crock Pot, mix the lentils with the thyme and the other ingredients, toss, put the lid on and cook on Low for 6 hours.
2. Divide between plates and serve as a side dish.

Nutrition Info:
- calories 200, fat 2, fiber 4, carbs 7, protein 8

Ramen Noodles

Servings: 5
Cooking Time: 25 Minutes

Ingredients:
- 1 tbsp ramen seasoning
- 10 oz. ramen noodles
- 4 cups chicken stock
- 1 tsp salt
- 3 tbsp soy sauce
- 1 tsp paprika
- 1 tbsp butter

Directions:
1. Add chicken stock, butter, ramen, paprika, noodles and all other ingredients to the Crock Pot.
2. Put the cooker's lid on and set the cooking time to 25 minutes on High settings.
3. Serve warm.

Nutrition Info:
- Per Serving: Calories: 405, Total Fat: 19.2g, Fiber: 6g, Total Carbs: 49.93g, Protein: 15g

White Beans Mix

Servings: 4
Cooking Time: 6 Hours

Ingredients:
- 1 celery stalk, chopped
- 2 garlic cloves, minced
- 1 carrot, chopped
- 1 cup veggie stock
- ½ cup canned tomatoes, crushed
- ½ teaspoon chili powder
- ½ tablespoon Italian seasoning
- 15 ounces canned white beans, drained
- 1 tablespoon parsley, chopped

Directions:
1. In your Crock Pot, mix the beans with the celery, garlic and the other ingredients, toss, put the lid on and cook on Low for 6 hours.
2. Divide the mix between plates and serve.

Nutrition Info:
- calories 223, fat 3, fiber 7, carbs 10, protein 7

Butter Glazed Yams

Servings: 7
Cooking Time: 4 Hrs.

Ingredients:
- 2 lb. yams, peeled and diced
- 5 tbsp butter, melted
- 5 oz. brown sugar
- 4 oz. white sugar
- ½ tsp salt
- 1 tsp vanilla extract
- 2 tbsp cornstarch

Directions:
1. Add melted butter, brown sugar, yams, white sugar, salt, and vanilla extract to the Crock Pot.
2. Put the cooker's lid on and set the cooking time to 4 hours on High settings.
3. Toss well, then stir in cornstarch, continue cooking for 10 minutes on High.
4. Mix well and serve.

Nutrition Info:
- Per Serving: Calories: 404, Total Fat: 16.4g, Fiber: 6g, Total Carbs: 63.33g, Protein: 3g

Italian Eggplant

Servings: 2
Cooking Time: 2 Hours

Ingredients:
- 2 small eggplants, roughly cubed
- ½ cup heavy cream
- Salt and black pepper to the taste
- 1 tablespoon olive oil
- A pinch of hot pepper flakes
- 2 tablespoons oregano, chopped

Directions:
1. In your Crock Pot, mix the eggplants with the cream and the other ingredients, toss, put the lid on and cook on High for 2 hours.
2. Divide between plates and serve as a side dish.

Nutrition Info:
- calories 132, fat 4, fiber 6, carbs 12, protein 3

Soups & Stews Recipes

Soups & Stews Recipes

Shredded Beef Soup

Servings: 8
Cooking Time: 8 1/2 Hours

Ingredients:
- 1 1/2 pounds beef roast
- 1 sweet onion, chopped
- 2 garlic cloves, chopped
- 2 carrots, sliced
- 2 celery stalks, sliced
- 2 red bell peppers, cored and diced
- 1/2 teaspoon cumin powder
- 1/2 teaspoon dried oregano
- 1/2 teaspoon dried basil
- 1/2 teaspoon chili powder
- 2 cups chicken stock
- 5 cups water
- 2 jalapenos, chopped
- 1 cup fire roasted tomatoes
- Salt and pepper to taste

Directions:
1. Combine the onion, garlic, carrots, celery, bell peppers, cumin powder, oregano, basil, chili powder, stock and water in your Crock Pot.
2. Add the jalapenos and tomatoes, as well as salt and pepper then place the beef in the center of the cooker, making sure it's covered in liquid.
3. Cook on low settings for 8 hours.
4. When done, shred the beef into fine threads and serve the soup warm.

Hungarian Goulash Soup

Servings: 8
Cooking Time: 8 1/2 Hours

Ingredients:
- 2 sweet onions, chopped
- 1 pound beef roast, cubed
- 2 tablespoons canola oil
- 2 carrots, diced
- 1/2 celery stalk, diced
- 2 red bell peppers, cored and diced
- 1 1/2 pounds potatoes, peeled and cubed
- 2 tablespoons tomato paste

- 1 cup diced tomatoes
- 1/2 cup beef stock
- 5 cups water
- 1/2 teaspoon cumin seeds
- 1/2 teaspoon smoked paprika
- Salt and pepper to taste

Directions:
1. Heat the oil in a skillet and stir in the beef. Cook for 5 minutes on all sides then stir in the onion. Sauté for 2 additional minutes then transfer in your Crock Pot.
2. Add the remaining ingredients and season with salt and pepper.
3. Cook on low settings for 8 hours.
4. Serve the soup warm.

Smoky Sweet Corn Soup

Servings: 6
Cooking Time: 5 1/2 Hours

Ingredients:
- 1 shallot, chopped
- 1 garlic clove, chopped
- 2 tablespoons olive oil
- 2 bacon slices, chopped
- 3 cups frozen corn
- 2 cups chicken stock
- 2 cups water
- 1/4 teaspoon chili powder
- Salt and pepper to taste

Directions:
1. Heat the oil in a skillet and add the garlic, shallot and bacon. Cook on all sides until golden then transfer in your Crock Pot.
2. Add the corn, stock, water and chili powder and season with salt and pepper.
3. Cook on low settings for 5 hours.
4. When done, puree the soup with an immersion blender and serve it warm.

White Chicken Chili Soup

Servings: 8
Cooking Time: 7 1/2 Hours

Ingredients:
- 1 pound ground chicken
- 2 tablespoons olive oil
- 1 yellow bell pepper, cored and diced
- 2 carrots, diced
- 1 celery stalk, diced
- 1 parsnip, diced
- 2 cans (15 oz.) white beans, drained
- 2 cups chicken stock
- 3 cups water
- 1/2 teaspoon chili powder
- Salt and pepper to taste

Directions:
1. Heat the oil in a skillet and stir in the chicken. Cook for 5 minutes, stirring often, then transfer the meat in your Crock Pot.
2. Add the remaining ingredients and season with salt and pepper.
3. Cover the pot and cook on low settings for 7 hours.
4. Serve the soup either warm or chilled.

Light Zucchini Soup

Servings:4
Cooking Time: 30 Minutes

Ingredients:
- 1 large zucchini
- 1 white onion, diced
- 4 cups beef broth
- 1 teaspoon dried thyme
- ½ teaspoon dried rosemary

Directions:
1. Pour the beef broth in the Crock Pot.
2. Add onion, dried thyme, and dried rosemary.
3. After this, make the spirals from the zucchini with the help of the spiralizer and transfer them in the Crock Pot.
4. Close the lid and cook the sou on High for 30 minutes.

Nutrition Info:
- InfoPer Serving: 64 calories, 6.2g protein, 6.5g carbohydrates, 1.6g fat, 1.6g fiber, 0mg cholesterol, 773mg sodium, 462mg potassium.

Chicken Taco Soup

Servings: 8
Cooking Time: 6 1/2 Hours

Ingredients:
- 4 chicken breasts, cut into strips
- 1 large onion, chopped
- 2 garlic cloves, chopped
- 1 can (15 oz.) pinto beans, drained
- 1 can (15 oz.) black beans, drained
- 1 cup diced tomatoes
- 1/2 cup canned corn, drained
- 1 cup dark beer
- 1 tablespoon Taco seasoning
- 2 cups chicken stock
- 4 cups water
- Salt and pepper to taste
- Tortilla chips for serving

Directions:
1. Combine the chicken, onion, garlic, beans and tomatoes in your Crock Pot.
2. Add the corn, beer, seasoning, stock and water then season with salt and pepper.
3. Cook the soup on low settings for 6 hours.
4. Serve the soup warm, topped with tortilla chips.

Moroccan Lamb Soup

Servings: 6
Cooking Time: 7 1/2 Hours

Ingredients:
- 1 pound lamb shoulder
- 1 teaspoon turmeric powder
- 1/2 teaspoon cumin powder
- 1/2 teaspoon chili powder
- 2 tablespoons canola oil
- 2 cups chicken stock
- 3 cups water
- 1 cup fire roasted tomatoes
- 1 cup canned chickpeas, drained
- 1 thyme sprig
- 1/2 teaspoon dried sage
- 1/2 teaspoon dried oregano
- Salt and pepper to taste
- 1 lemon, juiced

Directions:
1. Sprinkle the lamb with salt, pepper, turmeric, cumin powder and chili powder.

2. Heat the oil in a skillet and add the lamb. Cook on all sides for a few minutes then transfer it in a Crock Pot.
3. Add the remaining ingredients and season with salt and pepper.
4. Cook the soup on low settings for 7 hours.
5. Serve the soup warm.

Haddock Stew

Servings:6
Cooking Time: 3 Hours

Ingredients:
- ½ cup clam juice
- 2 teaspoons tomato paste
- 2 celery stalks, chopped
- ½ teaspoon ground coriander
- 14 oz haddock fillet, chopped
- 1 cup of water
- 1 teaspoon butter

Directions:
1. Melt the butter in the skillet and add chopped fish fillets.
2. Roast them for 1 minute per side and transfer in the Crock Pot.
3. Add celery stalk, ground coriander, clam juice, and tomato paste.
4. Then add water and close the lid.
5. Cook the stew on high for 3 hours.
6. Carefully stir the stew before serving.

Nutrition Info:
- InfoPer Serving: 92 calories, 16.3g protein, 2.7g carbohydrates, 1.3g fat, 0.2g fiber, 51mg cholesterol, 142mg sodium, 315mg potassium.

Sweet Potato & Sausage Soup

Servings: 6 (12.4 Ounces Per Serving)
Cooking Time: 7 Hours And 35 Minutes

Ingredients:
- 1 lb. sausage links, pork or chicken
- 8 large sweet potatoes, cubed
- 1 onion, chopped
- 1 glass red wine
- 4 tablespoons tomato sauce
- Olive oil
- 3 cups water
- Salt and pepper to taste and other seasonings

- 1 cup of bacon, cooked, cubed
- 1 cup smoked ham, cooked, cubed
- 1 red pepper, diced

Directions:
1. Chop the onion into cubes. Grease a frying pan and sauté onion until golden in color, for about six minutes. Add the cubed ham and bacon. Add cubed potatoes and salt and pepper to taste. Pour in wine and stir. Place all ingredients in Crock Pot. Add the water and cover and cook on LOW for 6-7 hours. Add the chopped pepper and tomato sauce and cook on LOW for an additional 30 minutes more. Serve hot.

Nutrition Info:
- Calories: 126.71, Total Fat: 2.02 g, Saturated Fat: 0.99 g, Cholesterol: 18.33 mg, Sodium: 787.22 mg, Potassium: 215.12 mg, Total Carbohydrates: 6.95 g, Fiber: 0.52 g, Sugar: 1.26 g, Protein: 15.3 g

Cabbage Stew

Servings:2
Cooking Time: 3 Hours

Ingredients:
- 2 cups white cabbage, shredded
- ½ cup tomato juice
- 1 teaspoon ground white pepper
- 1 cup cauliflower, chopped
- ½ cup potato, chopped
- 1 cup of water

Directions:
1. Put cabbage, potato, and cauliflower in the Crock Pot.
2. Add tomato juice, ground white pepper, and water. Stir the stew ingredients and close the lid.
3. Cook the stew on high for 3 hours.

Nutrition Info:
- InfoPer Serving: 57 calories, 2.8g protein, 13.3g carbohydrates, 0.2g fat, 3.9g fiber, 0mg cholesterol, 196mg sodium, 503mg potassium.

Basil Tomato Soup

Servings: 6
Cooking Time: 6 1/2 Hours

Ingredients:
- 2 tablespoons olive oil
- 2 red onions, sliced
- 1 teaspoon dried basil
- 1 1/2 pound fresh tomatoes, peeled and cubed
- 1 celery stalk, sliced
- 1/2 red chili, seeded and chopped
- 2 cups vegetable stock
- 2 cups water
- 1/2 cup half and half
- Salt and pepper to taste

Directions:
1. Heat the oil in a skillet and add the red onions. Cook on low heat for 10 minutes until softened.
2. Transfer in your Crock Pot and add the remaining ingredients, except the half and half.
3. Season with salt and pepper and cook on low settings for 6 hours.
4. When done, puree the soup with an immersion blender, adding the half and half as well.
5. Serve the soup warm.

Bacon Stew

Servings:4
Cooking Time: 5 Hours

Ingredients:
- 3 oz bacon, chopped, cooked
- 1/3 teaspoon ground black pepper
- ½ teaspoon garlic powder
- 2 cups vegetable stock
- 1 tablespoon cornstarch
- 1 cup turnip, peeled, chopped
- ½ cup carrot, chopped

Directions:
1. Mix cornstarch with vegetable stock and whisk until smooth.
2. Pour the liquid in the Crock Pot.
3. Add all remaining ingredients and close the lid.
4. Cook the stew on low for 5 hours.

Nutrition Info:
- InfoPer Serving: 142 calories, 8.6g protein, 6.4g carbohydrates, 9g fat, 1.3g fiber, 23mg cholesterol, 548mg sodium, 232mg potassium.

Sweet Corn Chowder

Servings: 8
Cooking Time: 6 1/4 Hours

Ingredients:
- 2 shallots, chopped
- 4 medium size potatoes, peeled and cubed1
- 1 celery stalk, sliced
- 1 can (15 oz.) sweet corn, drained
- 2 cups chicken stock
- 2 cups water
- Salt and pepper to taste

Directions:
1. Combine the shallot, potatoes, celery, corn, stock and water in a Crock Pot.
2. Add salt and pepper to taste and cook on low settings for 6 hours.
3. When done, remove a few tablespoons of corn from the pot then puree the remaining soup in the pot.
4. Pour the soup into serving bowls and top with the reserved corn.
5. Serve warm.

Snow Peas Soup

Servings:4
Cooking Time: 3.5 Hours

Ingredients:
- 1 tablespoon chives, chopped
- 1 teaspoon ground ginger
- 8 oz salmon fillet, chopped
- 5 oz bamboo shoots, canned, chopped
- 2 cups snow peas
- 1 teaspoon hot sauce
- 5 cups of water

Directions:
1. Put bamboo shoots in the Crock Pot.
2. Add ground ginger, salmon, snow peas, and water.
3. Close the lid and cook the soup for 3 hours on high.
4. Then add hot sauce and chives. Stir the soup carefully and cook for 30 minutes on high.

Nutrition Info:
- InfoPer Serving: 120 calories, 14.6g protein, 7.9g carbohydrates, 3.8g fat, 3.1g fiber, 25mg cholesterol, 70mg sodium, 612mg potassium

Tuscan Kale And White Bean Soup

Servings: 8
Cooking Time: 8 1/2 Hours

Ingredients:
- 1 1/2 cups dried white beans, rinsed
- 1 sweet onion, chopped
- 2 carrots, diced
- 1 celery stalk, sliced
- 1 teaspoon dried oregano
- 2 cups chicken stock
- 6 cups water
- 1 bay leaf
- 1 teaspoon dried basil
- 1 bunch kale, shredded
- Salt and pepper to taste
- 1 lemon, juiced

Directions:
1. Combine the beans, onion, carrots, celery, dried herbs, stock and water in your Crock Pot.
2. Add salt and pepper to taste and throw in the bay leaf as well.
3. Cook on low settings for 4 hours then add the kale and lemon juice and cook for 4 additional hours.
4. Serve the soup warm or chilled.

Meatball Tortellini Soup

Servings: 6
Cooking Time: 6 1/2 Hours

Ingredients:
- 1/2 pound ground chicken
- 1/4 cup white rice
- 1 garlic clove, chopped
- 1 tablespoon chopped parsley
- 2 cups chicken stock
- 4 cups water
- 1 celery stalk, sliced
- 1 carrot, sliced
- 1 shallot, chopped
- 6 oz. spinach tortellini
- Salt and pepper to taste

Directions:
1. Mix the chicken, rice, garlic, parsley, salt and pepper in a bowl.
2. Combine the stock, water, celery, carrot, shallot, salt and pepper in your Crock Pot.
3. Form small meatballs and drop them in the liquid.

4. Add the tortellini as well and cook on low settings for 6 hours.
5. Serve the soup warm and fresh.

Cream Of Chicken Soup

Servings: 6
Cooking Time: 7 1/2 Hours

Ingredients:
- 6 chicken thighs
- 6 cups water
- 1/4 cup all-purpose flour
- 1 cup chicken stock
- 1/4 teaspoon garlic powder
- 1 pinch chili flakes
- Salt and pepper to taste

Directions:
1. Combine the chicken with water and cook on low settings for 6 hours.
2. When done, remove the meat from the liquid and shred it off the bone.
3. Combine the flour with stock and mix well. Add the garlic powder and chili flakes and give it a good mix.
4. Pour this mixture over the liquid in the crock pot.
5. Add the meat and cook for 1 additional hour on high settings.
6. Serve the soup warm and fresh.

Snack Recipes

Snack Recipes

Tomato Mussels Salad

Servings: 4
Cooking Time: 1 Hour

Ingredients:
- 28 oz. canned tomatoes, crushed
- ½ cup white onion, chopped
- 2 jalapeno peppers, chopped
- ¼ cup dry white wine
- ¼ cup extra virgin olive oil
- ¼ cup balsamic vinegar
- 2 lbs. mussels, cleaned and scrubbed
- 2 tbsp red pepper flakes
- 2 garlic cloves, minced
- Salt to the taste
- ½ cup basil, chopped
- Lemon wedges for serving

Directions:
1. Add mussels, tomatoes and all other ingredients to the Crock Pot.
2. Put the cooker's lid on and set the cooking time to 1 hour on High settings.
3. Discard those mussels which remained unopened.
4. Serve the rest with lemon wedges.

Nutrition Info:
- Per Serving: Calories: 100, Total Fat: 1g, Fiber: 1g, Total Carbs: 7g, Protein: 2g

Cheesy Mix

Servings: 24
Cooking Time: 2 Hours

Ingredients:
- 2 cups small pretzels
- 2 cups wheat cereal
- 3 cups rice cereal
- 3 cups corn cereal
- 2 cups small cheese crackers
- 1/3 cup parmesan, grated
- 1/3 cup bacon flavor chips
- ½ cup melted butter
- 1/3 cup canola oil
- 1 ounce ranch dressing

Directions:
1. In your Crock Pot, mix pretzels with wheat cereal, rice cereal, corn cereal, crackers, chips and parmesan, cover and cook on High for 2 hours stirring every 20 minutes.
2. In a bowl, mix butter with oil and ranch dressing and whisk well.
3. Divide the mix from the Crock Pot into bowls and serve them with the ranch dressing on the side.

Nutrition Info:
- calories 182, fat 2, fiber 6, carbs 12, protein 4

Fava Bean Onion Dip

Servings: 6
Cooking Time: 5 Hours

Ingredients:
- 1 lb. fava bean, rinsed
- 1 cup yellow onion, chopped
- 4 and ½ cups of water
- 1 bay leaf
- ¼ cup olive oil
- 1 garlic clove, minced
- 2 tbsp lemon juice
- Salt to the taste

Directions:
1. Add 4 cups water, bay leaf, salt, and fava beans to the Crock Pot.
2. Put the cooker's lid on and set the cooking time to 3 hours on low settings.
3. Drain the Crock Pot beans and discard the bay leaf.
4. Return the cooked beans to the cooker and add onion, garlic, and ½ cup water.
5. Put the cooker's lid on and set the cooking time to 2 hours on Low settings.
6. Blend the slow-cooked beans with lemon juice and olive oil.
7. Serve.

Nutrition Info:
- Per Serving: Calories: 300, Total Fat: 3g, Fiber: 1g, Total Carbs: 20g, Protein: 6g

Fajita Dip

Servings: 6
Cooking Time: 4 Hours

Ingredients:
- 3 chicken breasts, skinless and boneless
- 8 ounces root beer
- 3 red bell peppers, chopped
- 1 yellow onion, chopped
- 8 ounces cream cheese
- 8 ounces pepper jack cheese, shredded
- 16 ounces sour cream
- 2 fajita seasoning mix packets
- 1 tablespoons olive oil
- Salt and black pepper to the taste

Directions:
1. In your Crock Pot, mix chicken with root beer, bell peppers, onion, cream cheese, pepper jack cheese, sour cream, fajita seasoning, oil, salt and pepper, stir, cover and cook on High for 4 hours.
2. Shred meat using2 forks, divide into bowls and serve.

Nutrition Info:
- calories 261, fat 4, fiber 6, carbs 17, protein 5

Peanut Bombs

Servings: 9
Cooking Time: 6 Hours

Ingredients:
- 1 cup peanut
- ½ cup flour
- 1 egg
- 1 tsp butter, melted
- 1 tsp salt
- 1 tsp turmeric
- 4 tbsp milk
- ¼ tsp nutmeg

Directions:
1. First, blend the peanuts in a blender then stir in flour.
2. Beat egg with milk, nutmeg, turmeric, and salt in a bowl.
3. Stir in the peanut-flour mixture and mix well to form a dough.
4. Grease the base of the Crock Pot with melted butter.
5. Divide the dough into golf ball-sized balls and

place them the cooker.
6. Put the cooker's lid on and set the cooking time to 6 hours on Low settings.
7. Serve.

Nutrition Info:
- Per Serving: Calories: 215, Total Fat: 12.7g, Fiber: 2g, Total Carbs: 17.4g, Protein: 10g

Ginger Chili Peppers

Servings: 7
Cooking Time: 3 Hours

Ingredients:
- 2 tbsp balsamic vinegar
- 10 oz. red chili pepper, chopped
- 4 garlic cloves, peeled and sliced
- 1 white onion, chopped
- 3 tbsp water
- 1 tsp oregano
- 1 tsp ground black pepper
- 4 tbsp olive oil
- 1 tsp ground nutmeg
- ½ tsp ground ginger

Directions:
1. Spread the red chili peppers in the Crock Pot.
2. Mix onion and garlic with remaining ingredients and spread on top of chili peppers.
3. Put the cooker's lid on and set the cooking time to 3 hours on High settings.
4. Serve.

Nutrition Info:
- Per Serving: Calories: 96, Total Fat: 8g, Fiber: 1g, Total Carbs: 5.87g, Protein: 1g

Lentils Salsa

Servings: 2
Cooking Time: 3 Hours

Ingredients:
- 1 cup canned lentils, drained
- 1 cup mild salsa
- 3 ounces tomato paste
- 2 tablespoons balsamic vinegar
- 1 small sweet onion, chopped
- 1 garlic clove, minced
- ½ tablespoon sugar
- A pinch of red pepper flakes
- A pinch of salt and black pepper
- 1 tablespoon chives, chopped

Directions:
1. In your Crock Pot, mix the lentils with the salsa and the other ingredients, toss, put the lid on and cook on High for 3 hours.
2. Divide into bowls and serve as a party salsa.

Nutrition Info:
- calories 260, fat 3, fiber 4, carbs 6, protein 7

Shrimp Salad

Servings: 2
Cooking Time: 2 Hours

Ingredients:
- ½ pound shrimp, peeled and deveined
- 1 green bell pepper, chopped
- ½ cup kalamata olives, pitted and halved
- 4 spring onions, chopped
- 1 red bell pepper, chopped
- ½ cup mild salsa
- 1 tablespoon olive oil
- 1 garlic clove, minced
- ¼ teaspoon oregano, dried
- ¼ teaspoon basil, dried
- Salt and black pepper to the taste
- A pinch of red pepper, crushed
- 1 tablespoon parsley, chopped

Directions:
1. In your Crock Pot, mix the shrimp with the peppers and the other ingredients, toss, put the lid on and cook on High for 2 hours.
2. Divide into bowls and serve as an appetizer.

Nutrition Info:
- calories 240, fat 2, fiber 5, carbs 7, protein 2

Caramel Corn

Servings: 13
Cooking Time: 2 Hours

Ingredients:
- ½ cup butter
- 1 teaspoon vanilla extract
- ¼ cup corn syrup
- 1 cup brown sugar
- 1 teaspoon baking soda
- 12 cups plain popcorn
- 1 cup mixed nuts
- Cooking spray

Directions:
1. Grease your Crock Pot with cooking spray, add butter, vanilla, corn syrup, brown sugar and baking soda, cover and cook on High for 1 hour, stirring after 30 minutes.
2. Add popcorn, toss, cover and cook on Low for 1 hour more.
3. Add nuts, toss, divide into bowls and serve as a snack.

Nutrition Info:
- calories 250, fat 14, fiber 1, carbs 20, protein 2

Black Bean Salsa Salad

Servings: 6
Cooking Time: 4 Hours

Ingredients:
- 1 tablespoon soy sauce
- ½ teaspoon cumin, ground
- 1 cup canned black beans
- 1 cup salsa
- 6 cups romaine lettuce leaves
- ½ cup avocado, peeled, pitted and mashed

Directions:
1. In your Crock Pot, mix black beans with salsa, cumin and soy sauce, stir, cover and cook on Low for 4 hours.
2. In a salad bowl, mix lettuce leaves with black beans mix and mashed avocado, toss and serve.

Nutrition Info:
- calories 221, fat 4, fiber 7, carbs 12, protein 3

Salsa Snack

Servings: 6
Cooking Time: 3 Hours

Ingredients:
- 10 roma tomatoes, chopped
- 2 jalapenos, chopped
- 1 sweet onion, chopped
- 28 ounces canned plum tomatoes
- 3 garlic cloves, minced
- 1 bunch cilantro, chopped
- Salt and black pepper to the taste

Directions:
1. In your Crock Pot, mix roma tomatoes with jalapenos, onion, plum tomatoes and garlic, stir, cover and cook on High for 3 hours.
2. Add salt, pepper and cilantro, stir, divide into bowls and serve cold.

Nutrition Info:
- calories 162, fat 4, fiber 6, carbs 12, protein 3

Lemony Artichokes

Servings: 4 (5.2 Ounces Per Serving)
Cooking Time: 4 Hours And 10 Minutes

Ingredients:
- 4 artichokes
- 2 tablespoons coconut butter, melted
- 3 tablespoons lemon juice
- 1 teaspoon sea salt
- Ground black pepper to taste

Directions:
1. Wash the artichokes. Pull off the outermost leaves until you get to the lighter yellow leaves. Cut off the top third or so of the artichokes. Trim the bottom of the stems. Place in Crock-Pot. Mix together lemon juice, salt, and melted coconut butter and pour over artichokes. Cover and cook on LOW for 6-8 hours or on HIGH for 3-4 hours. Serve.

Nutrition Info:
- Calories: 113.58, Total Fat: 5.98 g, Saturated Fat: 3.7 g, Cholesterol: 15.27 mg, Sodium: 702.59 mg, Potassium: 487.2 mg, Total Carbohydrates: 8.25 g, Fiber: 6.95 g, Sugar: 1.56 g, Protein: 4.29 g

Cashew Dip

Servings: 10
Cooking Time: 3 Hours

Ingredients:
- 1 cup water
- 1 cup cashews
- 10 ounces hummus
- ¼ teaspoon garlic powder
- ¼ teaspoon onion powder
- A pinch of salt and black pepper
- ¼ teaspoon mustard powder
- 1 teaspoon apple cider vinegar

Directions:
1. In your Crock Pot, mix water with cashews, salt and pepper, stir, cover and cook on High for 3 hours.
2. Transfer to your blender, add hummus, garlic powder, onion powder, mustard powder and vinegar, pulse well, divide into bowls and serve.

Nutrition Info:
- calories 192, fat 7, fiber 7, carbs 12, protein 4

Lasagna Dip

Servings: 10
Cooking Time: 1 Hour

Ingredients:
- 8 ounces cream cheese
- ¾ cup parmesan, grated
- 1 and ½ cups ricotta
- ½ teaspoon red pepper flakes, crushed
- 2 garlic cloves, minced
- 3 cups marinara sauce
- 1 and ½ cups mozzarella, shredded
- 1 and ½ teaspoon oregano, chopped

Directions:
1. In your Crock Pot, mix cream cheese with parmesan, ricotta, pepper flakes, garlic, marinara, mozzarella and oregano, stir, cover and cook on High for 1 hour.
2. Stir, divide into bowls and serve as a dip.

Nutrition Info:
- calories 231, fat 4, fiber 7, carbs 21, protein 5

Beef And Chipotle Dip

Servings: 10
Cooking Time: 2 Hours

Ingredients:
- 8 ounces cream cheese, soft
- 2 tablespoons yellow onion, chopped
- 2 tablespoons mayonnaise
- 2 ounces hot pepper Monterey Jack cheese, shredded
- ¼ teaspoon garlic powder
- 2 chipotle chilies in adobo sauce, chopped
- 2 ounces dried beef, chopped
- ¼ cup pecans, chopped

Directions:
1. In your Crock Pot, mix cream cheese with onion, mayo, Monterey Jack cheese, garlic powder, chilies and dried beef, stir, cover and cook on Low for 2 hours.
2. Add pecans, stir, divide into bowls and serve.

Nutrition Info:
- calories 130, fat 11, fiber 1, carbs 3, protein 4

Beef Tomato Meatballs

Servings: 8
Cooking Time: 8 Hrs

Ingredients:
- 1 and ½ lbs. beef, ground
- 1 egg, whisked
- 16 oz. canned tomatoes, crushed
- 14 oz. canned tomato puree
- ¼ cup parsley, chopped
- 2 garlic cloves, minced
- 1 yellow onion, chopped
- Salt and black pepper to the taste

Directions:
1. Mix beef with parsley, egg, garlic, onion, and black pepper in a bowl.
2. Make 16 small meatballs out of this beef mixture.
3. Add tomato puree, tomatoes, and meatballs to the Crock Pot.
4. Put the cooker's lid on and set the cooking time to 8 hours on Low settings.
5. Serve warm.

Nutrition Info:
- Per Serving: Calories: 160, Total Fat: 5g, Fiber: 3g, Total Carbs: 10g, Protein: 7g

Dessert Recipes

Dessert Recipes

Raspberry Nutmeg Cake

Servings: 8
Cooking Time: 7 Hrs.

Ingredients:
- 4 eggs
- 1 cup sugar
- 1 cup flour
- 1 tsp vanilla extract
- 1 cup raspberry
- 1/3 cup sugar, brown
- 1 tbsp butter
- ¼ tsp nutmeg
- 1 tbsp cornstarch

Directions:
1. Separate the egg yolks from egg whites and keep them in a separate bowl.
2. Beat egg yolks with sugar, vanilla extract, cornstarch and nutmeg in a mixer.
3. Now beat the egg whites in an electric mixer until it forms peaks.
4. Add this egg white foam to the egg yolk mixture.
5. Mix gently, then add brown sugar and raspberry and blend again.
6. Grease the insert of your Crock Pot with butter.
7. Spread the raspberry batter in the cooker.
8. Put the cooker's lid on and set the cooking time to 7 hours on Low settings.
9. Slice and serve when chilled.

Nutrition Info:
- Per Serving: Calories: 234, Total Fat: 6.5g, Fiber: 6g, Total Carbs: 37.51g, Protein: 6g

Banana Muffins

Servings:2
Cooking Time: 2.5 Hours

Ingredients:
- 2 eggs, beaten
- 2 bananas, chopped
- 4 tablespoons flour
- ½ teaspoon vanilla extract
- ½ teaspoon baking powder

Directions:
1. Mash the chopped bananas and mix them with eggs.
2. Then add vanilla extract and baking powder.
3. Add flour and stir the mixture until smooth.
4. Pour the banana mixture in the muffin molds (fill ½ part of every muffin mold) and transfer in the Crock Pot.
5. Cook the muffins on High for 2.5 hours.

Nutrition Info:
- InfoPer Serving: 229 calories, 84g protein, 39.9g carbohydrates, 4.9g fat, 3.5g fiber, 164mg cholesterol, 64mg sodium, 626mg potassium.

Matcha Shake

Servings:4
Cooking Time: 40 Minutes

Ingredients:
- 1 teaspoon matcha green tea
- 2 cups of coconut milk
- 2 bananas, mashed
- ¼ cup agave nectar

Directions:
1. Mix agave nectar with coconut milk and matcha green tea. Mix the mixture until smooth and pour it in the Crock Pot.
2. Cook the mixture on high for 40 minutes.
3. Then transfer the mixture in the blender, add mashed bananas and blend the liquid until smooth.
4. Pour the cooked shake in the glasses and cool to room temperature.

Nutrition Info:
- InfoPer Serving: 359 calories, 3.4g protein, 28.3g carbohydrates, 28.8g fat, 4.7g fiber, 0mg cholesterol, 19mg sodium, 527mg potassium.

Vegan Mousse

Servings:3
Cooking Time: 2 Hours

Ingredients:
- 1 cup of coconut milk
- 2 tablespoons corn starch
- 1 teaspoon vanilla extract
- 1 avocado, pitted, pilled

Directions:
1. Mix coconut milk and corn starch until smooth and pour in the Crock Pot.
2. Add vanilla extract and cook it on High for 2 hours.
3. Then cool the mixture till room temperature and mix with avocado.
4. Blend the mousse until fluffy and smooth.

Nutrition Info:
- InfoPer Serving: 348 calories, 3.1g protein, 16.4g carbohydrates, 32.1g fat, 6.3g fiber, 0mg cholesterol, 16mg sodium, 537mg potassium.

Almond Bars

Servings:6
Cooking Time: 2 Hours

Ingredients:
- 1 tablespoon cocoa powder
- ½ cup flour
- ½ cup coconut flour
- 4 tablespoons coconut oil
- 1 teaspoon baking powder
- 2 oz almonds, chopped
- ¼ cup of sugar
- 2 eggs, beaten

Directions:
1. Mix all ingredients in the bowl and knead the smooth dough.
2. The put the dough in the Crock Pot, flatten it, and cut into bars.
3. Close the lid and cook the dessert on High for 2 hours.

Nutrition Info:
- InfoPer Serving: 266 calories, 6.4g protein, 26g carbohydrates, 16.5g fat, 5.8g fiber, 55mg cholesterol, 22mg sodium, 206mg potassium.

Spiced Peach Crisp

Servings: 6
Cooking Time: 3.5 Hrs.

Ingredients:
- 1 lb. peaches, pitted and sliced
- ¼ cup of sugar
- 4 tbsp lemon juice
- 1 tsp vanilla extract
- 5 oz oats
- 1 tsp baking soda
- 1 tsp vinegar
- 1/3 cup flour
- 3 tbsp butter
- 1 tsp ground ginger
- ½ tsp pumpkin pie seasoning

Directions:
1. Grease the insert of Crock Pot with butter.
2. Place the peach slices in the insert and top them with sugar and lemon juice.
3. Toss oats with vanilla extract, vinegar, baking soda, flour, ground ginger, pumpkin pie seasoning in a bowl.
4. Spread this oats spice mixture on top of the peaches.
5. Put the cooker's lid on and set the cooking time to 1.5 hours on High settings.
6. Remove the lid and stir the cooked mixture well.
7. Cover again and continue cooking for another 2 hours on High settings.
8. Serve.

Nutrition Info:
- Per Serving: Calories: 212, Total Fat: 7.6g, Fiber: 5g, Total Carbs: 41.26g, Protein: 5g

Amaretti Cheesecake

Servings: 8
Cooking Time: 6 1/2 Hours

Ingredients:
- Crust:
- 6 oz. Amaretti cookies, crushed
- 1/4 cup butter, melted
- Filling:
- 24 oz. cream cheese
- 1/2 cup sour cream
- 4 eggs
- 1/2 cup white sugar
- 1 tablespoon vanilla extract
- 1 tablespoon Amaretto liqueur

Directions:
1. Mix the crushed cookies with butter then transfer the mix in your crock pot and press it well on the bottom of the pot.
2. For the filling, mix the cream cheese, sour cream, eggs, sugar, vanilla and liqueur and give it a quick mix.
3. Pour the filling over the crust and cook for 6 hours on low settings.
4. Allow the cheesecake to cool before slicing and serving.

Pumpkin Cheesecake

Servings: 8
Cooking Time: 6 1/2 Hours

Ingredients:
- Crust:
- 8 oz. graham crackers, crushed
- 1/2 cup butter, melted
- Filling:
- 24 oz. cream cheese
- 1 1/2 cups pumpkin puree
- 3 eggs
- 2 tablespoons cornstarch
- 1/2 cup white sugar
- 1 teaspoon vanilla extract
- 1/2 teaspoon cinnamon powder
- 1/2 teaspoon ground ginger
- 1 pinch salt

Directions:
1. For the crust, mix the crackers with butter then transfer this mixture in your crock pot and press it

well.
2. For the filling, combine all the ingredients in a bowl and mix well. Pour this mixture over the crust and cook on low settings for 6 hours.
3. Allow the cheesecake to cool in the pot before slicing and serving.

Raisin Bake

Servings:4
Cooking Time: 6 Hours

Ingredients:
- 1 cup cottage cheese
- 2 oz raisins, chopped
- 1 egg, beaten
- 3 tablespoons sugar, powdered
- 1 teaspoon vanilla extract
- 1 teaspoon peanuts, chopped

Directions:
1. The Crock Pot with baking paper.
2. Then mix all ingredients in the bowl and mix until smooth.
3. Transfer the mixture in the Crock Pot and flatten the surface of it well.
4. Close the lid and cook the bake on Low for 6 hours.

Nutrition Info:
- InfoPer Serving: 150 calories, 9.8g protein, 22.6g carbohydrates, 2.6g fat, 0.6g fiber, 45mg cholesterol, 247mg sodium, 182mg potassium.

Creamy Dark Chocolate Dessert

Servings: 6
Cooking Time: 1 Hr.

Ingredients:
- ½ cup heavy cream
- 4 oz. dark chocolate, unsweetened and chopped

Directions:
1. Add cream with chocolate in the insert of Crock Pot.
2. Put the cooker's lid on and set the cooking time to 1 hour on High settings.
3. Allow this mixture to cool.
4. Serve.

Nutrition Info:
- Per Serving: Calories: 78, Total Fat: 1g, Fiber: 1g, Total Carbs: 2g, Protein: 1g

Milk Fondue

Servings:3
Cooking Time: 4 Hours

Ingredients:
- 5 oz milk chocolate, chopped
- 1 tablespoon butter
- 1 teaspoon vanilla extract
- ¼ cup milk

Directions:
1. Put the chocolate in the Crock Pot in one layer.
2. Then top it with butter, vanilla extract, and milk.
3. Close the lid and cook the dessert on Low for 4 hours.
4. Gently stir the cooked fondue and transfer in the ramekins.

Nutrition Info:
- InfoPer Serving: 301 calories, 4.3g protein, 29.3g carbohydrates, 18.3g fat, 1.6g fiber, 23mg cholesterol, 74mg sodium, 191mg potassium.

Raisin-flax Meal Bars

Servings: 8
Cooking Time: 3.5 Hrs.

Ingredients:
- ¼ cup raisins
- 1 cup oat flour
- 1 egg, whisked
- 4 oz banana, mashed
- 5 oz milk
- 1 tbsp flax meal
- 1 tsp ground cinnamon
- ½ tsp baking soda
- 1 tbsp lemon juice
- 1 tbsp butter
- 1 tbsp flour

Directions:
1. Whisk egg with mashed banana, oat flour, milk, flax meal, raising in a bowl.
2. Stir in cinnamon, lemon juice, baking soda, and flour, then knead well.
3. Grease the insert of the Crock Pot with butter.
4. Make big balls out of this raisin dough and shape them into 3-4 inches bars.
5. Place these bars in the insert of the Crock Pot.
6. Put the cooker's lid on and set the cooking time to 3 hours on Low settings.

7. Serve when chilled.

Nutrition Info:
- Per Serving: Calories: 152, Total Fat: 3.7g, Fiber: 2g, Total Carbs: 26.74g, Protein: 4g

Browned Butter Pumpkin Cheesecake

Servings: 8
Cooking Time: 6 1/2 Hours

Ingredients:
- Crust:
- 1 1/4 cups crushed graham crackers
- 1/2 cup butter
- Filling:
- 1 cup pumpkin puree
- 24 oz. cream cheese
- 4 eggs
- 1/2 cup light brown sugar
- 1 pinch salt
- 1 teaspoon cinnamon powder
- 1 teaspoon ground ginger
- 1/2 teaspoon cardamom powder
- 1/4 cup butter

Directions:
1. To make the curst, start by browning the butter. Place the butter in a saucepan and cook for a few minutes until it starts to look golden. Allow to cool slightly.
2. Mix the browned butter with crushed crackers then transfer the mixture in your crock pot and press it well on the bottom of the pot.
3. For the filling, brown 1/4 cup butter as described above then stir in the pumpkin puree, cream cheese, eggs, sugar, salt, cinnamon, ginger and cardamom.
4. Pour the mixture over the curst and cook on low settings for 6 hours.
5. Allow the cheesecake to cool down before slicing and serving.

Quinoa Pudding

Servings: 2
Cooking Time: 2 Hours

Ingredients:
- 1 cup quinoa
- 2 cups almond milk
- ½ cup sugar
- ½ tablespoon walnuts, chopped
- ½ tablespoon almonds, chopped

Directions:
1. In your Crock Pot, mix the quinoa with the milk and the other ingredients, toss, put the lid on and cook on High for 2 hours.
2. Divide the pudding into cups and serve.

Nutrition Info:
- calories 213, fat 4, fiber 6, carbs 10, protein 4

Apple, Avocado And Mango Bowls

Servings: 2
Cooking Time: 2 Hours

Ingredients:
- 1 cup avocado, peeled, pitted and cubed
- 1 cup mango, peeled and cubed
- 1 apple, cored and cubed
- 2 tablespoons brown sugar
- 1 cup heavy cream
- 1 tablespoon lemon juice

Directions:
1. In your Crock Pot, combine the avocado with the mango and the other ingredients, toss gently, put the lid on and cook on Low for 2 hours.
2. Divide the mix into bowls and serve.

Nutrition Info:
- calories 60, fat 1, fiber 2, carbs 20, protein 1

Banana Ice Cream

Servings:2
Cooking Time: 5 Hours

Ingredients:
- ½ cup cream
- 4 tablespoons sugar
- 4 bananas, chopped
- 2 egg yolks

Directions:
1. Mix sugar with egg yolks and blend until you get a lemon color mixture.
2. After this, mix the cream with egg yolks and transfer in the Crock Pot.
3. Cook the mixture on low for 5 hours. Stir the liquid from time to time.
4. After this, mix the cream mixture with bananas and blend until smooth.
5. Place the mixture in the plastic vessel and refrigerate until solid.

Nutrition Info:
- InfoPer Serving: 392 calories, 5.8g protein, 80.4g carbohydrates, 8.6g fat, 6.1g fiber, 221mg cholesterol, 30mg sodium, 885mg potassium.

No Crust Lemon Cheesecake

Servings: 8
Cooking Time: 6 1/4 Hours

Ingredients:
- 24 oz. cream cheese
- 1 lemon, zested and juiced
- 2 tablespoons cornstarch
- 1/2 cup white sugar
- 4 eggs
- 1 teaspoon vanilla extract
- 1/4 cup butter, melted

Directions:
1. Mix all the ingredients in a bowl.
2. Pour the cheesecake mix in a greased Crock Pot and cook on low settings for 6 hours.
3. Allow the cheesecake to cool in the pot before slicing and serving.

APPENDIX A: Measurement Conversions

BASIC KITCHEN CONVERSIONS & EQUIVALENTS

DRY MEASUREMENTS CONVERSION CHART

3 TEASPOONS = 1 TABLESPOON = 1/16 CUP

6 TEASPOONS = 2 TABLESPOONS = 1/8 CUP

12 TEASPOONS = 4 TABLESPOONS = 1/4 CUP

24 TEASPOONS = 8 TABLESPOONS = 1/2 CUP

36 TEASPOONS = 12 TABLESPOONS = 3/4 CUP

48 TEASPOONS = 16 TABLESPOONS = 1 CUP

METRIC TO US COOKING CONVERSIONS

OVEN TEMPERATURES

120 °C = 250 °F

160 °C = 320 °F

180° C = 350 °F

205 °C = 400 °F

220 °C = 425 °F

LIQUID MEASUREMENTS CONVERSION CHART

8 FLUID OUNCES = 1 CUP = 1/2 PINT = 1/4 QUART

16 FLUID OUNCES = 2 CUPS = 1 PINT = 1/2 QUART

32 FLUID OUNCES = 4 CUPS = 2 PINTS = 1 QUART

 = 1/4 GALLON

128 FLUID OUNCES = 16 CUPS = 8 PINTS = 4 QUARTS = 1 GALLON

BAKING IN GRAMS

1 CUP FLOUR = 140 GRAMS

1 CUP SUGAR = 150 GRAMS

1 CUP POWDERED SUGAR = 160 GRAMS

1 CUP HEAVY CREAM = 235 GRAMS

VOLUME

1 MILLILITER = 1/5 TEASPOON

5 ML = 1 TEASPOON

15 ML = 1 TABLESPOON

240 ML = 1 CUP OR 8 FLUID OUNCES

1 LITER = 34 FL. OUNCES

US TO METRIC COOKING CONVERSIONS

1/5 TSP = 1 ML

1 TSP = 5 ML

1 TBSP = 15 ML

1 FL OUNCE = 30 ML

1 CUP = 237 ML

1 PINT (2 CUPS) = 473 ML

1 QUART (4 CUPS) = .95 LITER

1 GALLON (16 CUPS) = 3.8 LITERS

1 OZ = 28 GRAMS

1 POUND = 454 GRAMS

BUTTER

1 CUP BUTTER = 2 STICKS = 8 OUNCES = 230 GRAMS = 8 TABLESPOONS

WHAT DOES 1 CUP EQUAL

1 CUP = 8 FLUID OUNCES

1 CUP = 16 TABLESPOONS

1 CUP = 48 TEASPOONS

1 CUP = 1/2 PINT

1 CUP = 1/4 QUART

1 CUP = 1/16 GALLON

1 CUP = 240 ML

WEIGHT

1 GRAM = .035 OUNCES

100 GRAMS = 3.5 OUNCES

500 GRAMS = 1.1 POUNDS

1 KILOGRAM = 35 OUNCES

BAKING PAN CONVERSIONS

1 CUP ALL-PURPOSE FLOUR = 4.5 OZ

1 CUP ROLLED OATS = 3 OZ 1 LARGE EGG = 1.7 OZ

1 CUP BUTTER = 8 OZ 1 CUP MILK = 8 OZ

1 CUP HEAVY CREAM = 8.4 OZ

1 CUP GRANULATED SUGAR = 7.1 OZ

1 CUP PACKED BROWN SUGAR = 7.75 OZ

1 CUP VEGETABLE OIL = 7.7 OZ

1 CUP UNSIFTED POWDERED SUGAR = 4.4 OZ

BAKING PAN CONVERSIONS

9-INCH ROUND CAKE PAN = 12 CUPS

10-INCH TUBE PAN =16 CUPS

11-INCH BUNDT PAN = 12 CUPS

9-INCH SPRINGFORM PAN = 10 CUPS

9 X 5 INCH LOAF PAN = 8 CUPS

9-INCH SQUARE PAN = 8 CUPS

Appendix B : Recipes Index

C

I

J

K

L

M

S

T

V

W

Y

Z

Made in the USA
Las Vegas, NV
09 October 2024

96578126R00050